HALLOWEEN SPOOKTACULAR

37 GRAVEST HITS

Cherry Lane Music Company
Director of Publications/Project Editor: Mark Phillips

ISBN 978-1-60378-386-6

Addams Family Theme

Theme from the TV Show and Movie

Music and Lyrics by
Vic Mizzy

Moderately

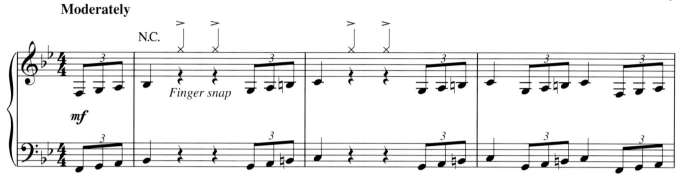

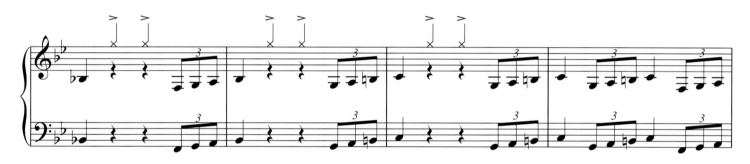

They're creep - y and they're kook - y, mys - te - ri - ous and spook - y, they're

al - to - geth - er ook - y, the Ad-dams Fam - i - ly. Their house is a mu - se - um, where

peo - ple come to see 'em, they real - ly are a scree-um, the Ad-dams Fam - i - ly.

(Spoken:) Neat. Sweet.

Petite. So get a witch - 's shawl on, a broom - stick you can crawl on, we're

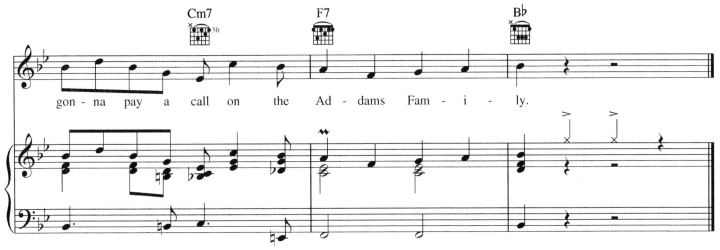

gon - na pay a call on the Ad - dams Fam - i - ly.

Theme from Buffy the Vampire Slayer

By Charles Dennis, Parry Gripp
and Stephen Sherlock

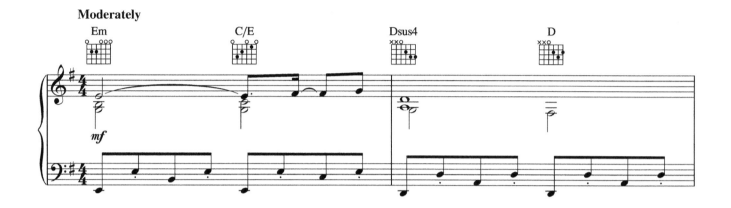

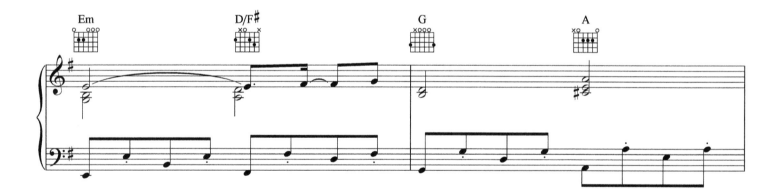

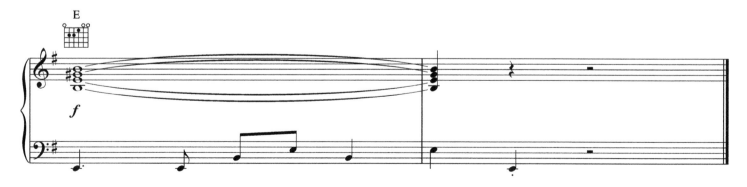

Ding-Dong! The Witch Is Dead

from THE WIZARD OF OZ

Lyric by E.Y. "Yip" Harburg

Music by Harold Arlen

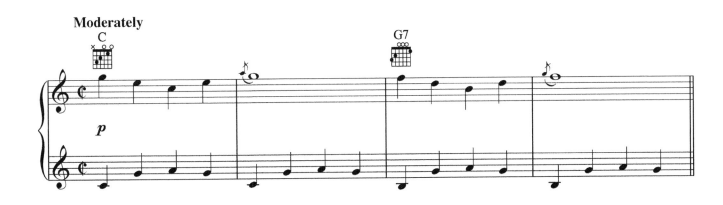

Once there was a wick - ed witch in the love - ly land of Oz, and a

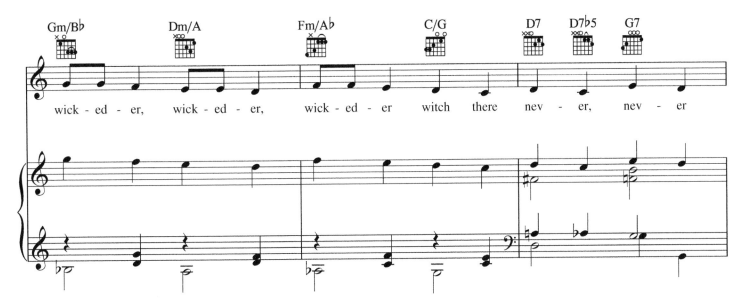

wick - ed - er, wick - ed - er, wick - ed - er witch there nev - er, nev - er

was. She filled the folks in Munch-kin land with ter-ror and with

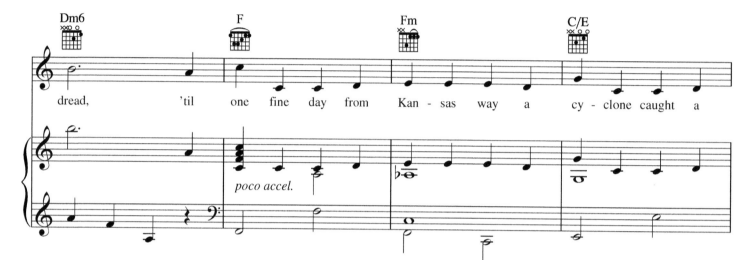

dread, 'til one fine day from Kan-sas way a cy-clone caught a

poco accel.

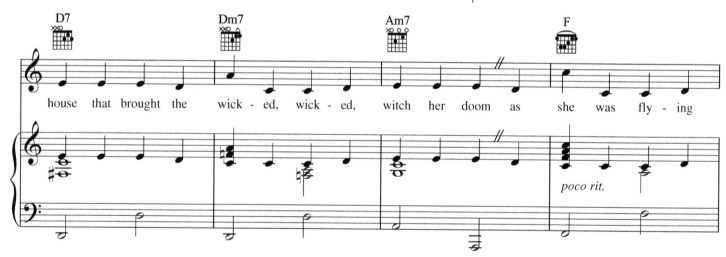

house that brought the wick-ed, wick-ed, witch her doom as she was fly-ing

poco rit.

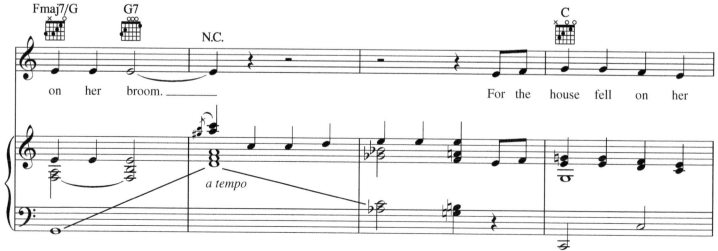

on her broom. _____ For the house fell on her

N.C.

a tempo

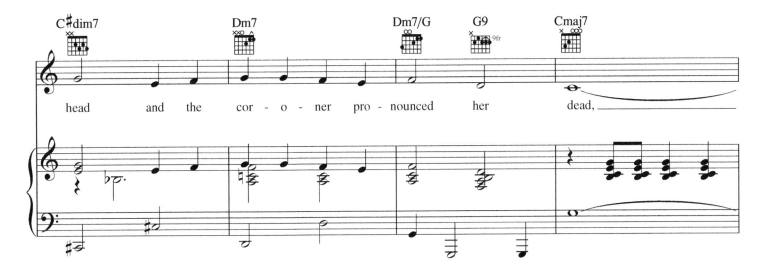

head and the cor - o - ner pro - nounced her dead,

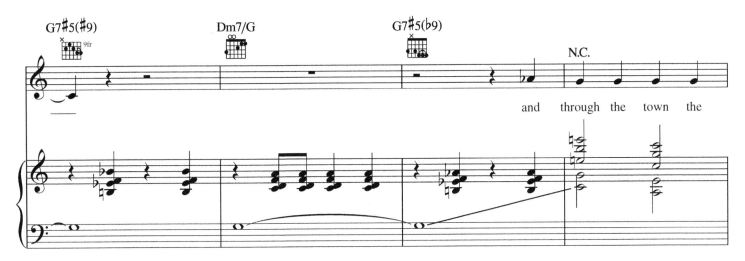

and through the town the

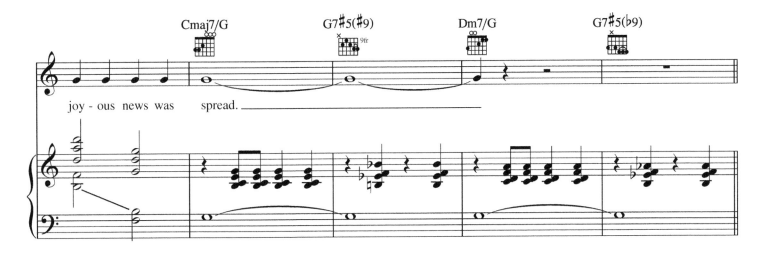

joy - ous news was spread.

Ding -- dong, the witch is dead! Which old witch? The wick - ed witch.

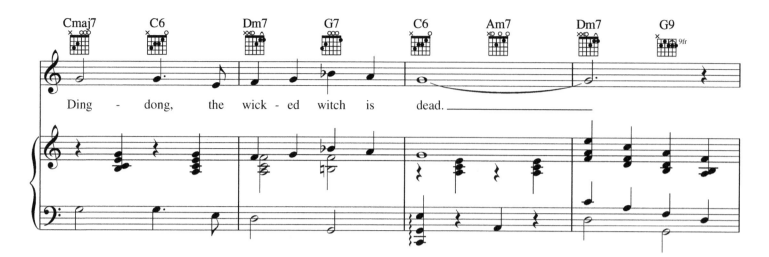

Ding - dong, the wick - ed witch is dead. _____

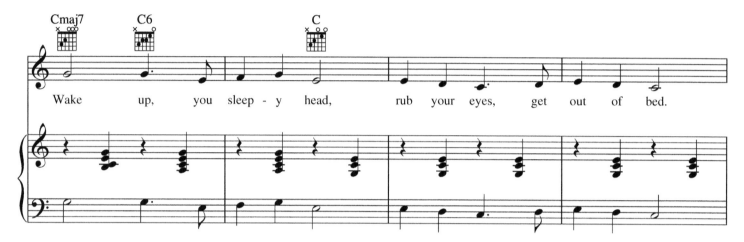

Wake up, you sleep - y head, rub your eyes, get out of bed.

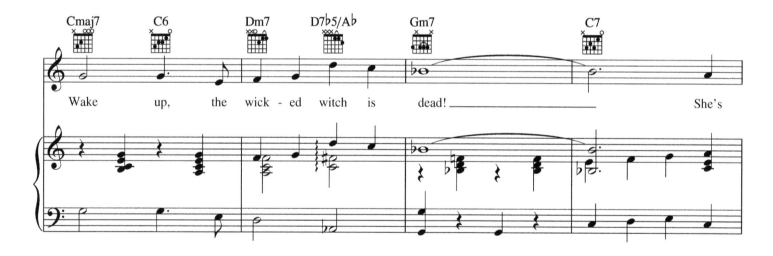

Wake up, the wick - ed witch is dead! _____ She's

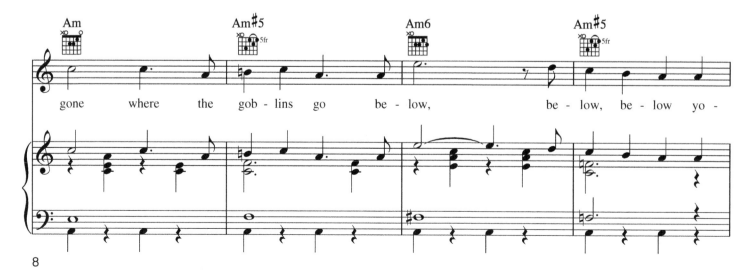

gone where the gob - lins go be - low, be - low, be - low yo -

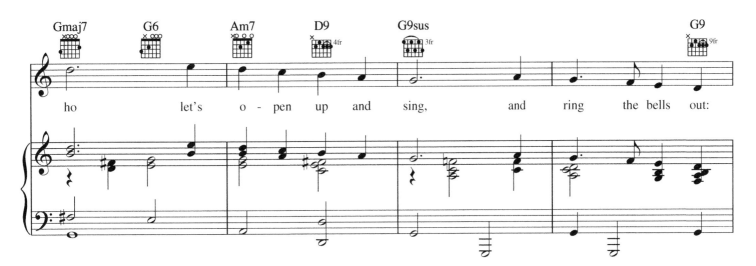

ho   let's o - pen up and sing,   and   ring   the bells out:

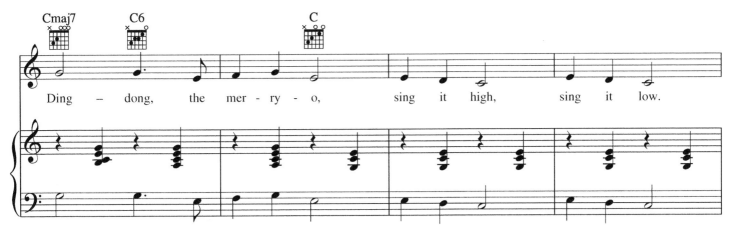

Ding — dong,   the   mer - ry - o,   sing   it   high,   sing   it   low.

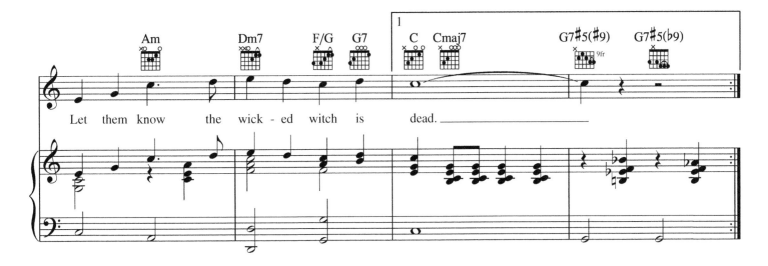

Let them know   the   wick - ed   witch   is   dead. _____

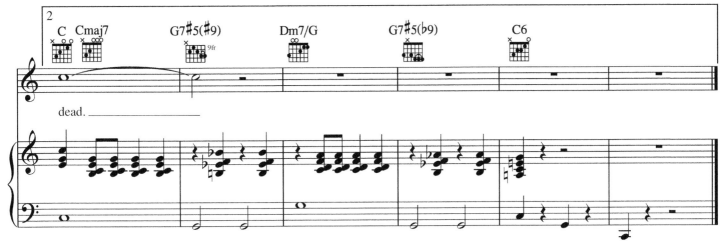

dead. _____

Casper the Friendly Ghost

from the Paramount Cartoon

Words by Mack David

Music by Jerry Livingston

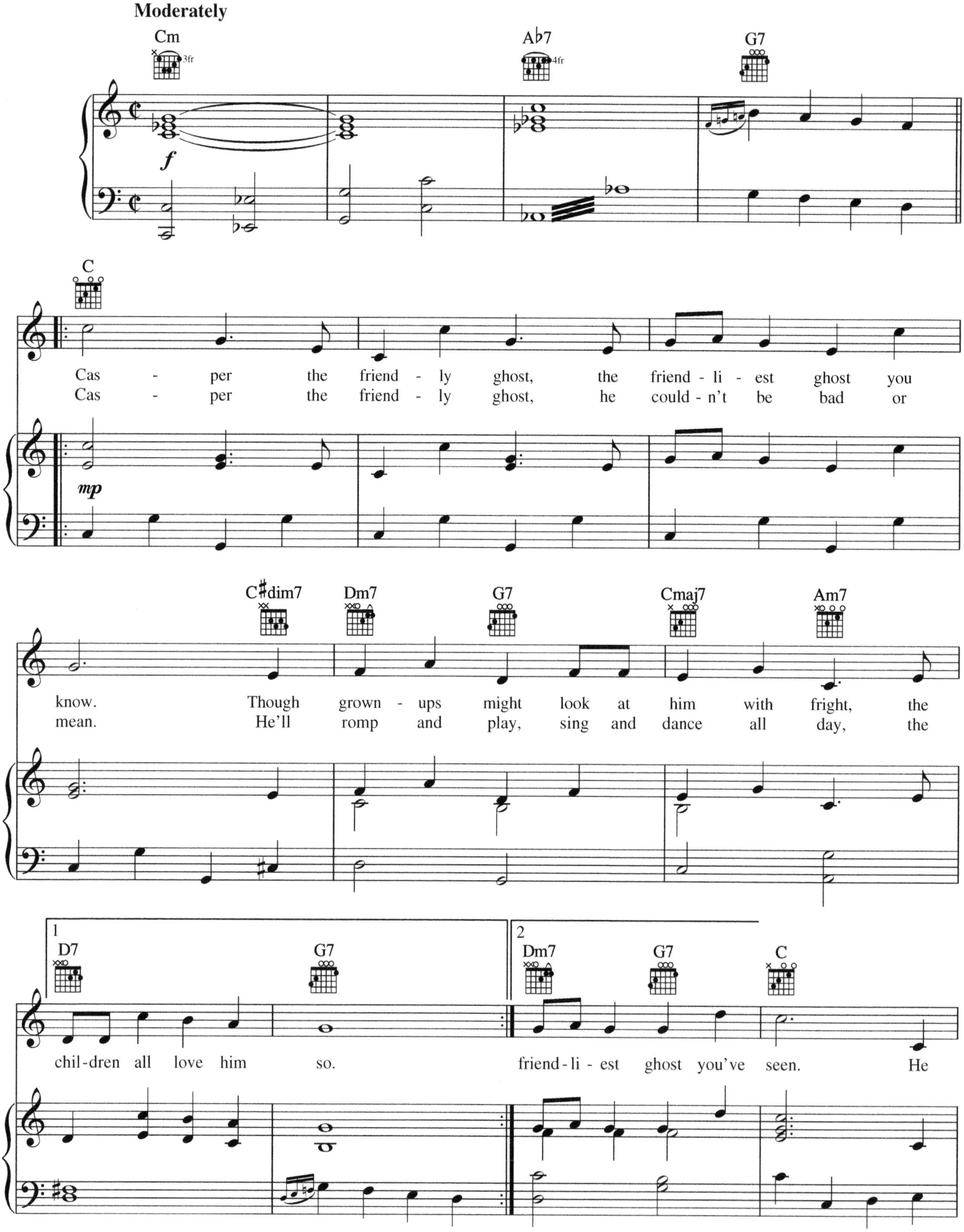

Moderately
Cm
3fr
A♭7
4fr
G7
f
C
mp
Cas - per the friend - ly ghost, the friend - li - est ghost you
Cas - per the friend - ly ghost, he could - n't be bad or
C♯dim7
Dm7
G7
Cmaj7
Am7
know. Though grown - ups might look at him with fright, the
mean. He'll romp and play, sing and dance all day, the
1
D7
G7
chil - dren all love him so.
2
Dm7
G7
C
friend - li - est ghost you've seen. He

al - ways says "Hel - lo," and he's real - ly glad to meet cha. Wher -

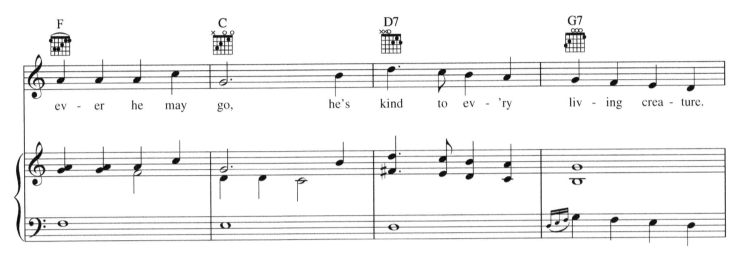

ev - er he may go, he's kind to ev - 'ry liv - ing crea - ture.

Grown - ups don't un - der - stand why chil - dren love him the most, but

kids all know that he loves them so, Cas - per the friend - ly ghost.

Dinner with Drac

Words and Music by
Kevin McDaniels

A din-ner was served __ for three at Drac-u-la's house, by the sea.

The hors d'oeuvres were fine, but I choked on my wine __ when I learned

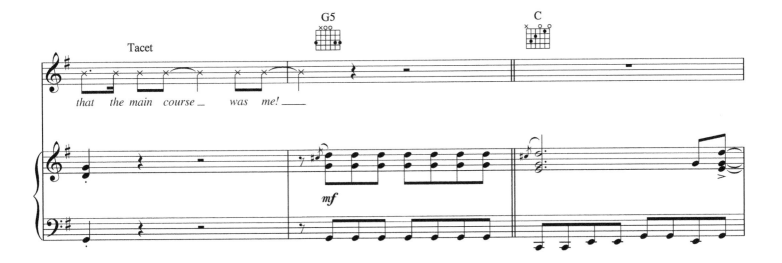

Tacet

that the main course __ was me! __

I - gor,   *the scal-pels go on the*

13

left, with the pitch - forks! I - gor, I - gor...

What a swim-mer is Drac-u - la's daugh-ter. But her

pool looks more red _____ than it ought-a. The blood stains the boat,

but it's eas - y to float 'cause blood is much thick - er than wa - ter!

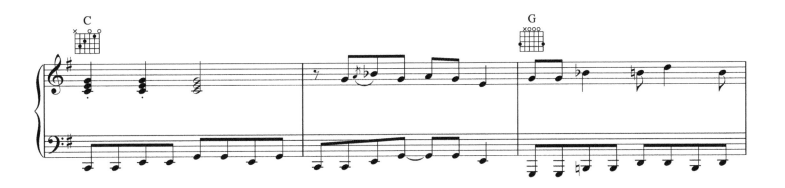

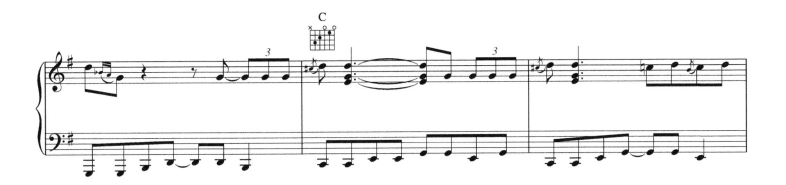

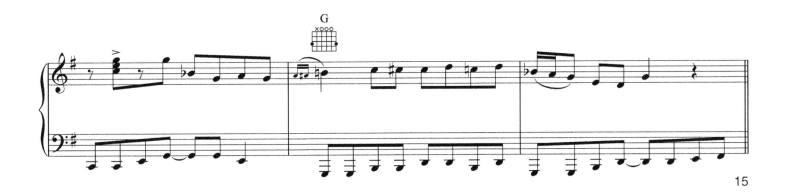

Drac - u - la, old friend, how are things in Tran - syl -

va - nia? Ha, ha, ha, ha...

For des - sert, there was bat - wing con - fet - ti and the veins of a mum - my ___ named Bet - ty.

I first frowned up - on it, but with ketch - up on it, it tast - ed

ver - y much like spa - ghet - ti! Ha, ha, ha, ha...

Ha, ha, ha, ha...

Good - night, _ wher - ev - er you are!

Begin fade   *Fade out*

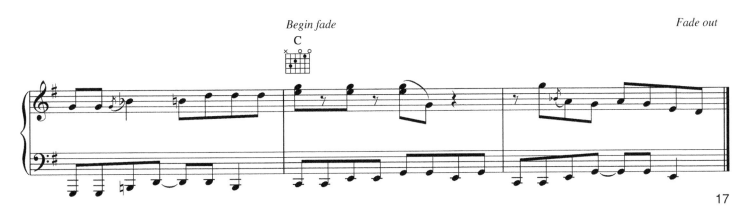

Don't Fear the Reaper

Words and Music by
Donald Roeser

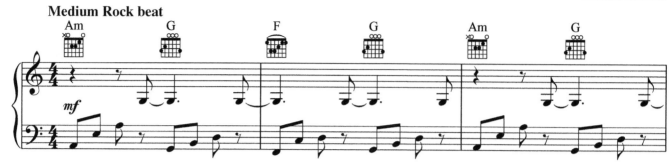

All our times have

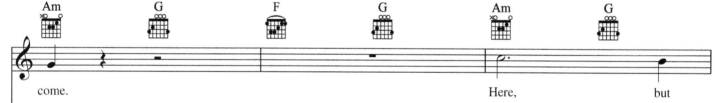

come.   Here,   but

now   they're   gone.

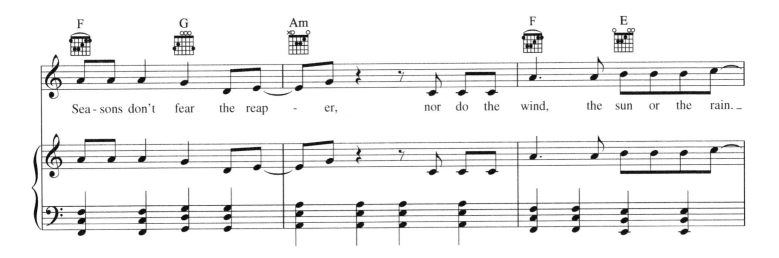

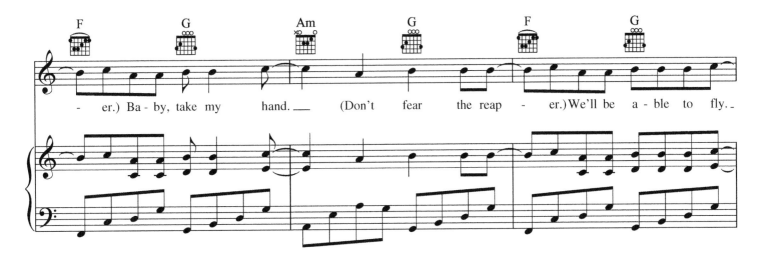

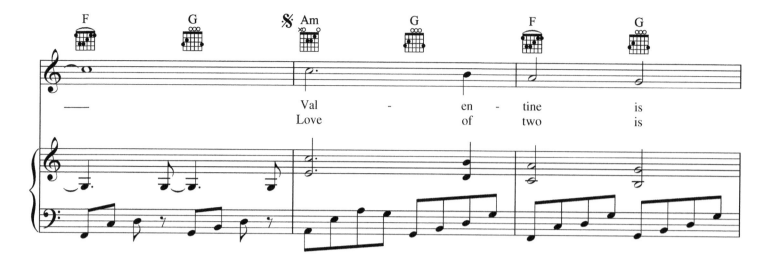

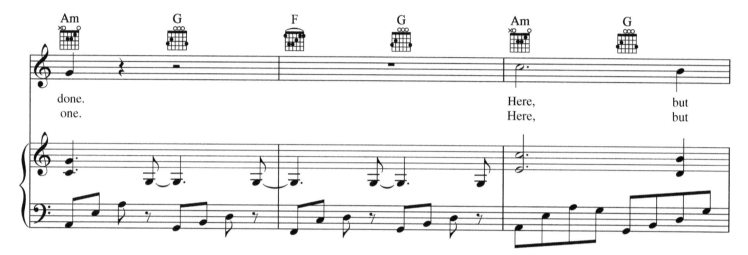

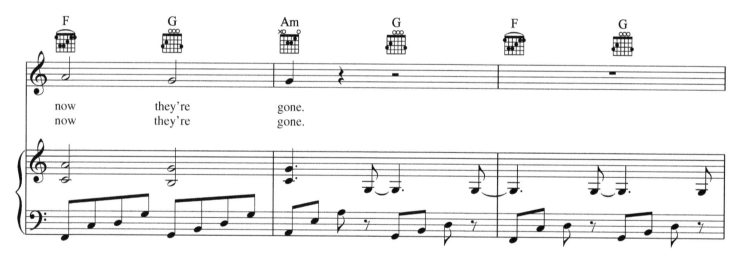

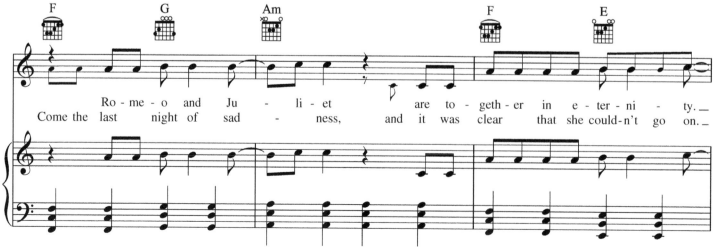

Then the door was o-pen, and the wind ap peared. The

For - ty thou-sand men and wom-en ev - 'ry day.

Ro - me - o and Ju - li - et.

Like Ro - me - o and Ju -

For - ty thou - sand men and wom-en ev - 'ry day. An -

can - dles blew and then dis - ap - peared. The

- li - et.

Re - de - fine hap -

oth - er for - ty thou sand com - in' ev - 'ry day. Come on, ba -

cur - tains flew, and then he ap peared. Come on, ba -

- pi - ness.

{ We can be like they ___ are.
{ Say - ing, don't be a - fraid. _____

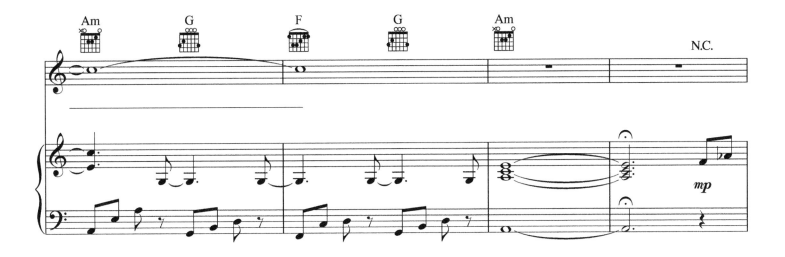

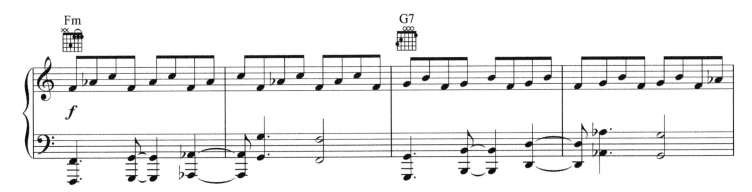
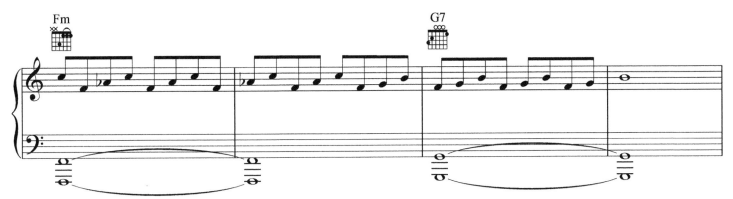

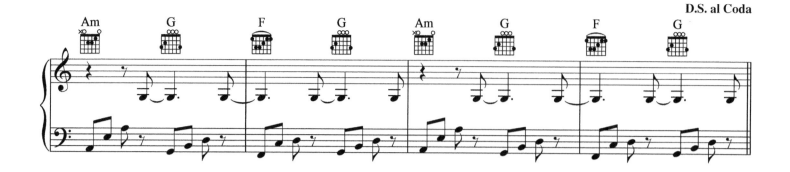

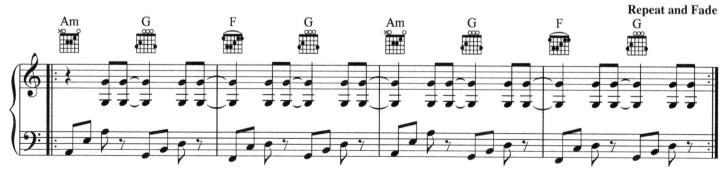

Theme from "Dracula"

from DRACULA

Music by
John Williams

Moderately

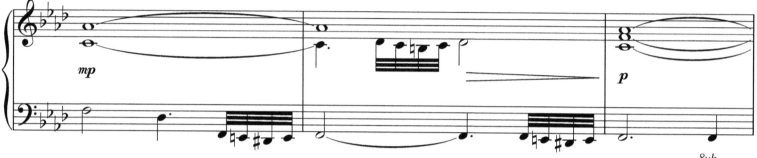

26

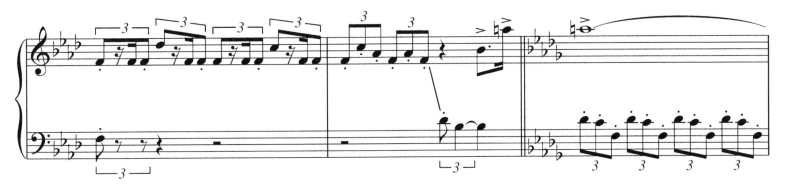

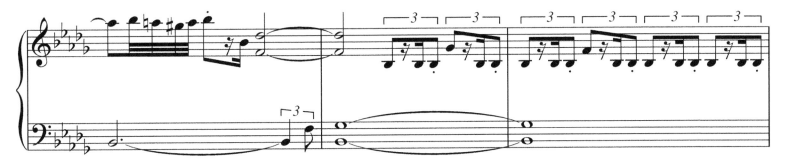

The Fog

from the John Carpenter Productions Motion Picture
JOHN CARPENTER'S THE FOG

Music by
John Carpenter

Moderately

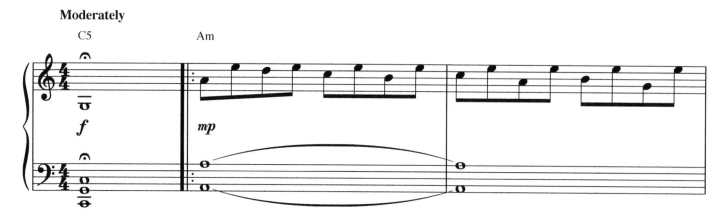

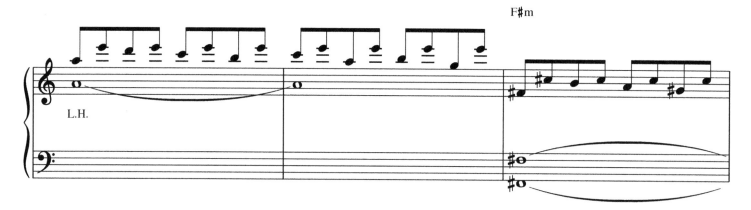

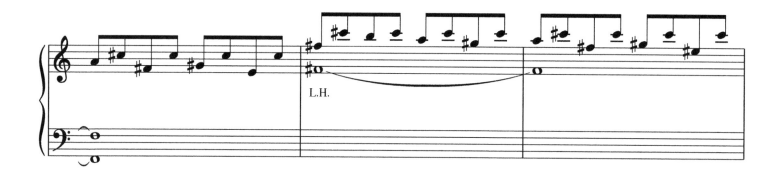

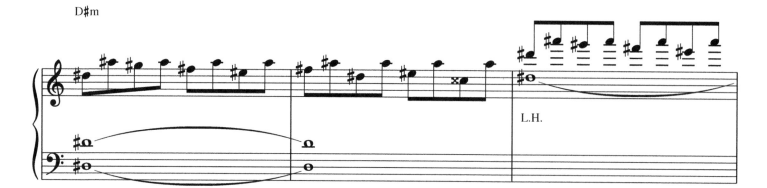

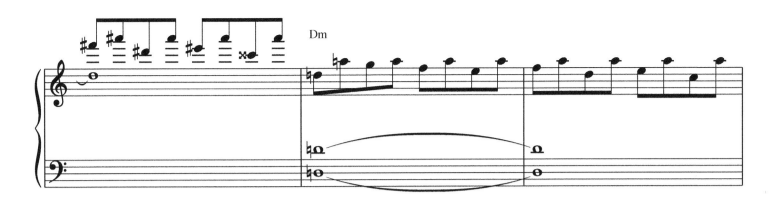

Dm

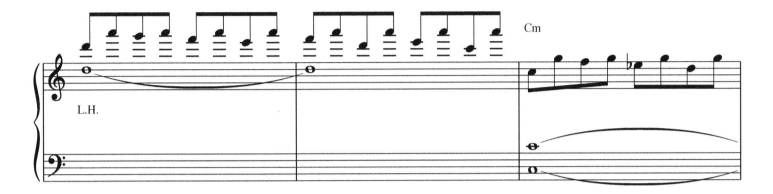

Cm

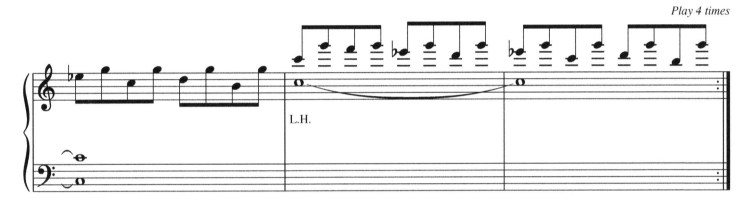

Play 4 times

Am

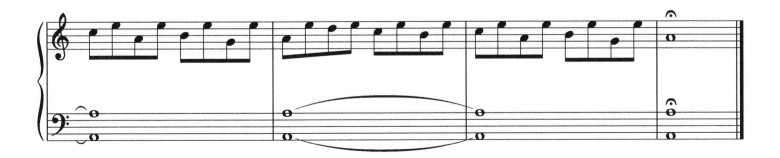

Frankenstein

By Edgar Winter

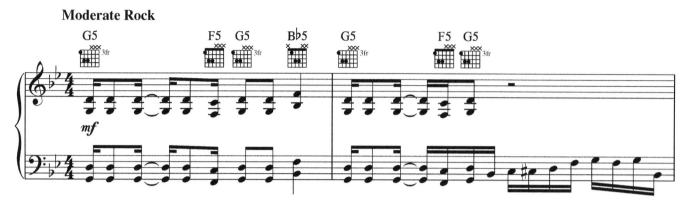

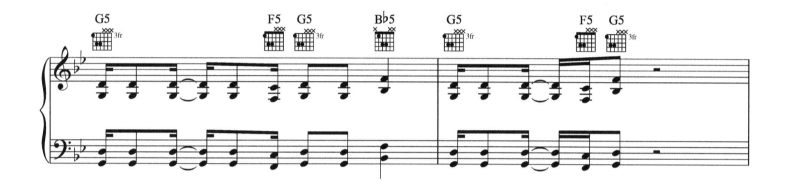

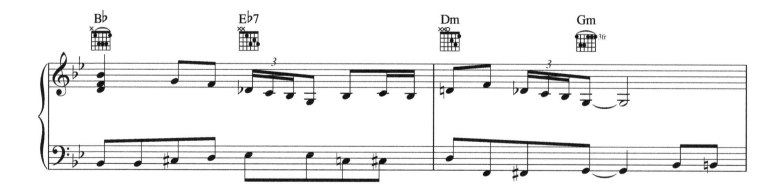

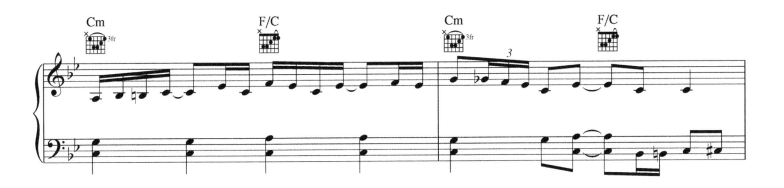

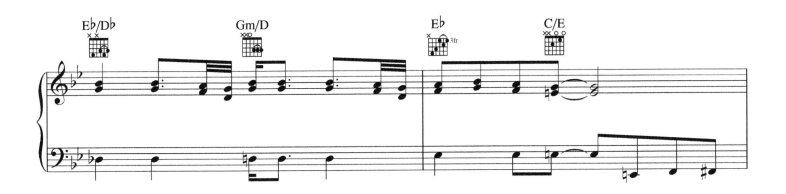

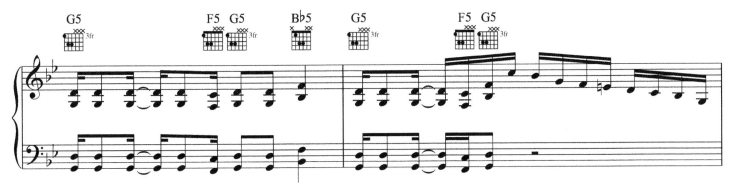

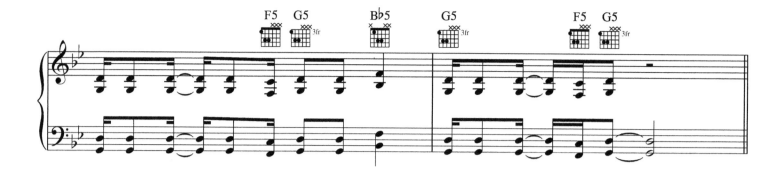

Instrumental solo

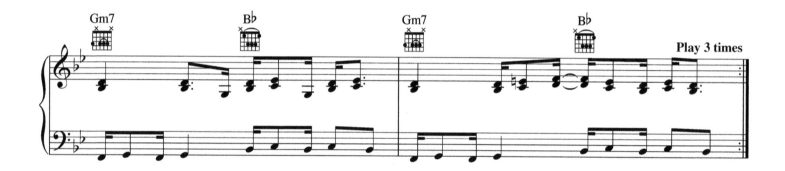

Play 3 times

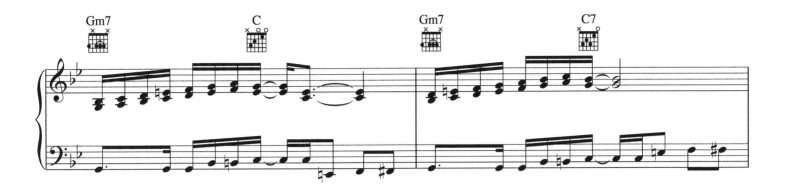

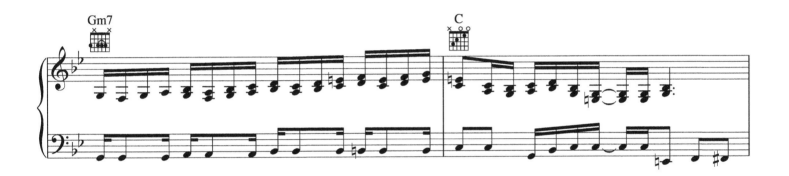

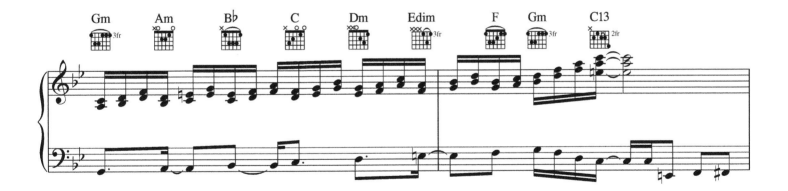

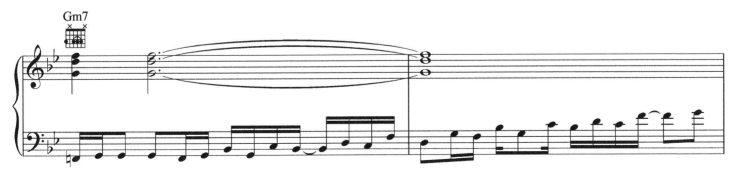

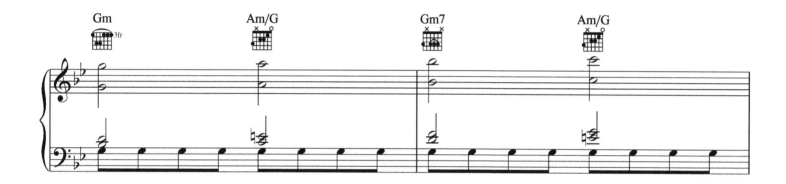

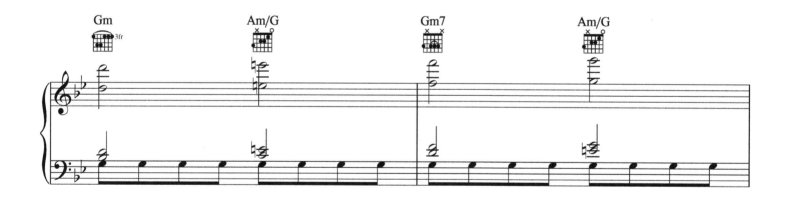

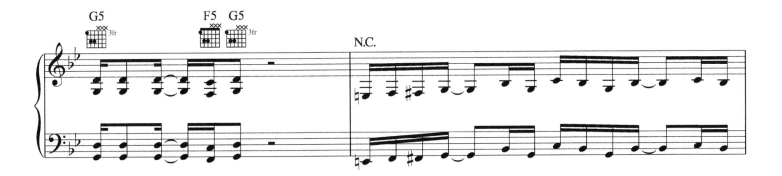

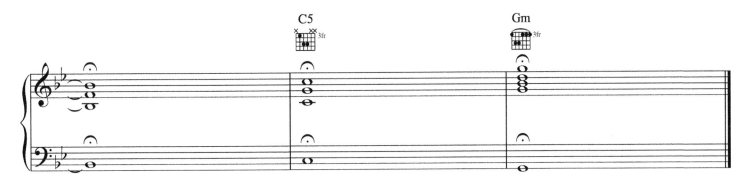

Friday the 13th Theme

Written by
Harry Manfredini

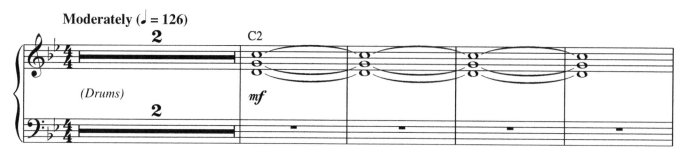

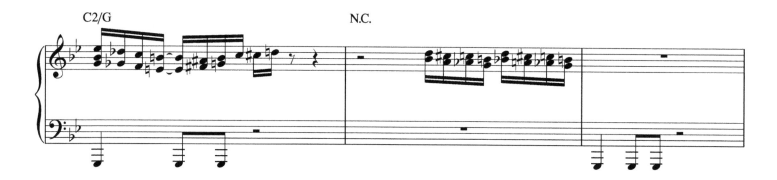

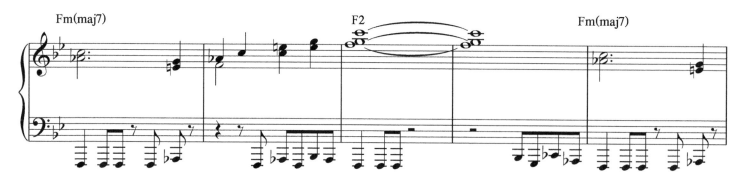

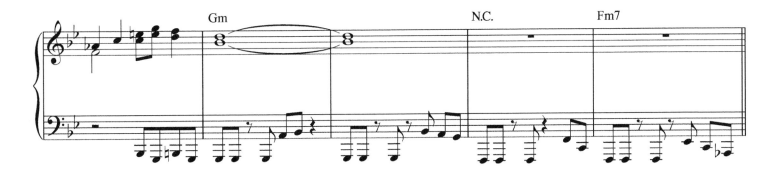

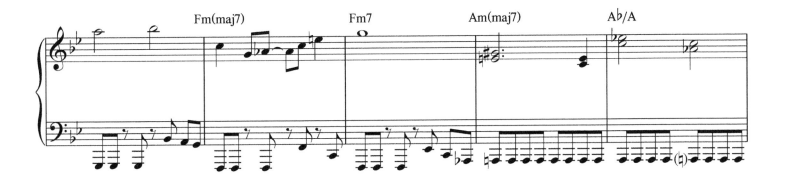

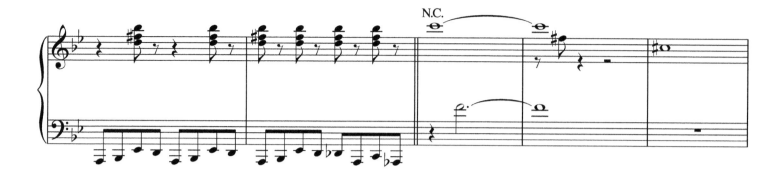

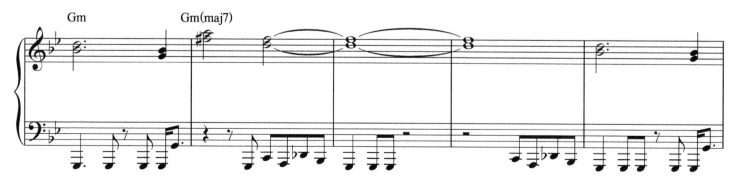

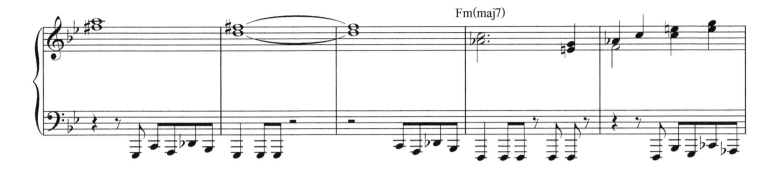

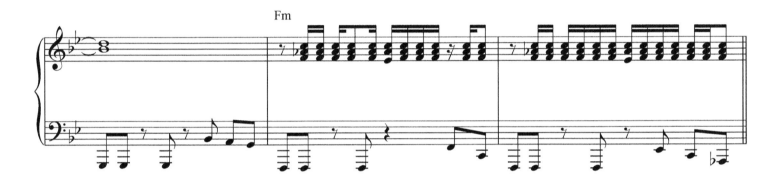

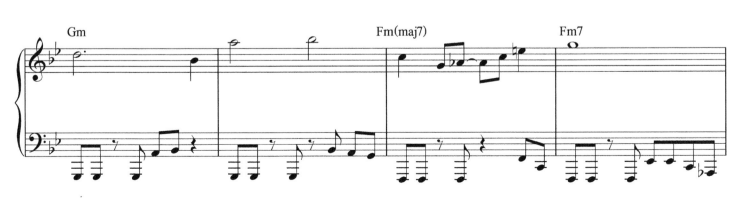

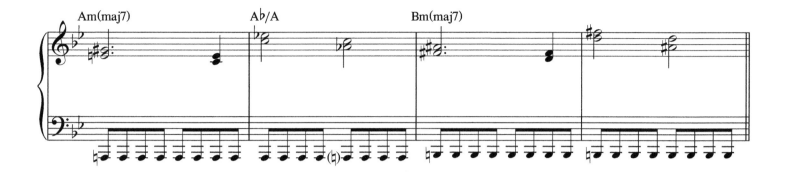

Repeat and Fade

Ghostbusters

from the Columbia Motion Picture GHOSTBUSTERS

Words and Music by
Ray Parker, Jr.

who you gon-na call? Ghost - bust - ers!

I ain't 'fraid_ of no ghost!

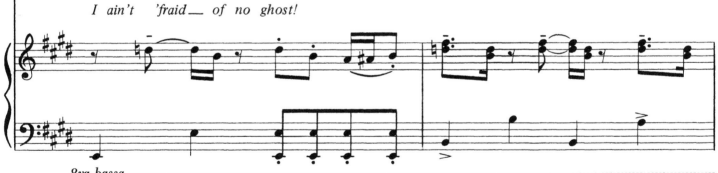

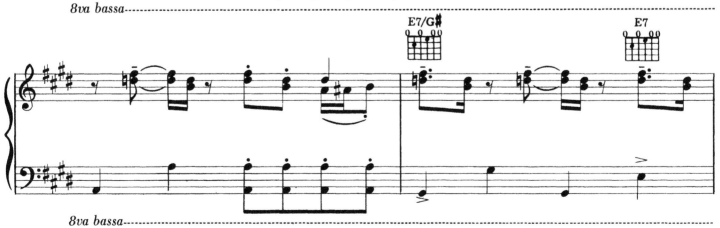

8va bassa----------

I ain't 'fraid___ of no ghost!

2. If you're   I ain't 'fraid___ of no ghost!

8va bassa

Chorus:

I hear it likes the girls...

I ain't 'fraid — of no ghost!

E7   E/A

D.S. al Coda I

Yeah,   yeah,   yeah,   yeah.

Coda I

N.C.

8va b ⌐

8va b ⌐

46

Bust - in' makes me feel good!

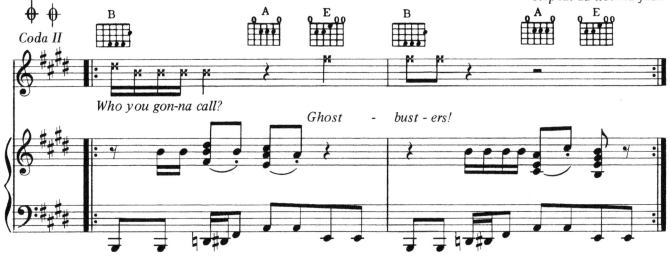

Repeat ad lib. and fade

Coda II

Who you gon-na call?   *Ghost - bust - ers!*

Verse 2:
Who you gonna call? (Ghostbusters!)
Mm, if you have a ghost of a freaky ghost baby, you'd better call ghostbusters!

Verse 3:
Don't get caught alone, oh no! (Ghostbusters!)
When it comes through your door,
Unless you just want some more, you'd better call ghostbusters!

Funeral March

from PIANO SONATA NO. 2, THIRD MOVEMENT

By Fryderyk Chopin

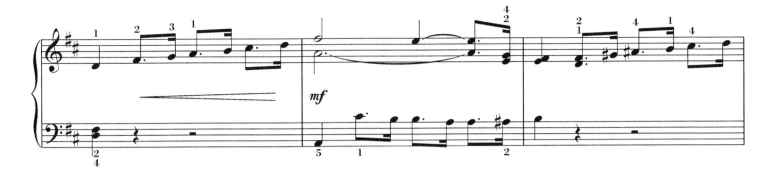

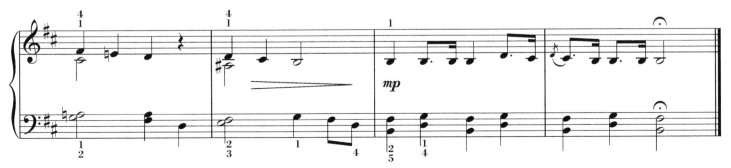

Funeral March of a Marionette

By Charles Gounod

Moderately fast, in 2

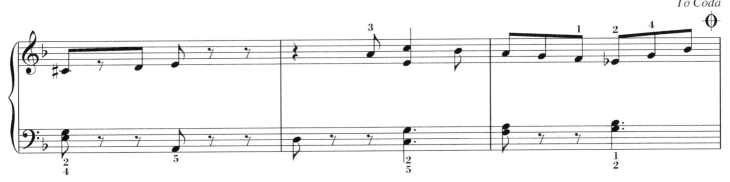

To Coda

D.S. al Coda

Coda

Haunted House

Words and Music by
Robert Geddins

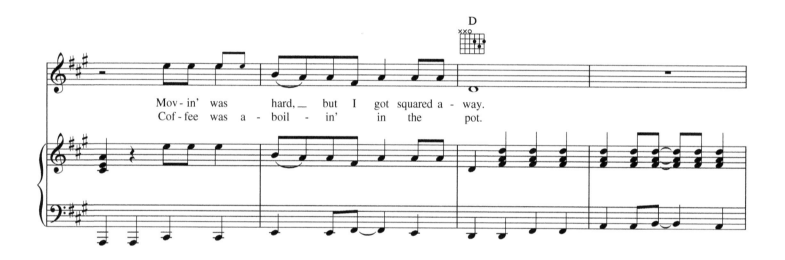

Tacet

Knew I'd moved in a haunt-ed house.
Had a hunk of meat in my hand.

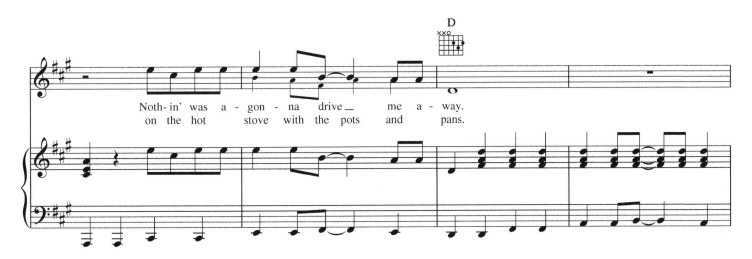

Tacet

Still, I made up my mind to stay.
From out of space there sat a man

Noth-in' was a - gon - na drive me a - way.
on the hot stove with the pots and pans.

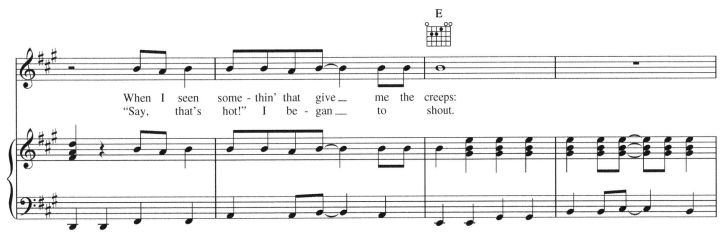

When I seen some-thin' that give me the creeps:
"Say, that's hot!" I be-gan to shout.

had one big eye _____ and _____ two big feet.
Drank the hot cof - fee right _____ from the spout.

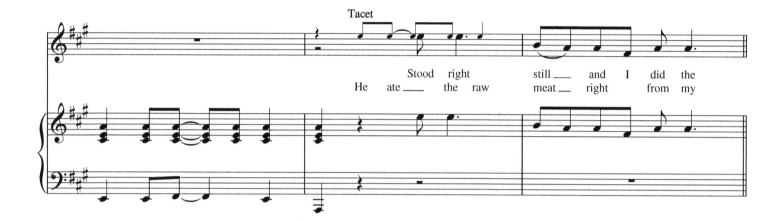

Stood right still _____ and I did the
He ate _____ the raw meat _____ right from my

freeze.
hand.

He did the stroll _____ right up to
Drank the hot grease _____ from the fry - in'

me.
pan.

Made a noise with his feet that sound _____ like a
Looked at me, said, "You _____ bet - ter

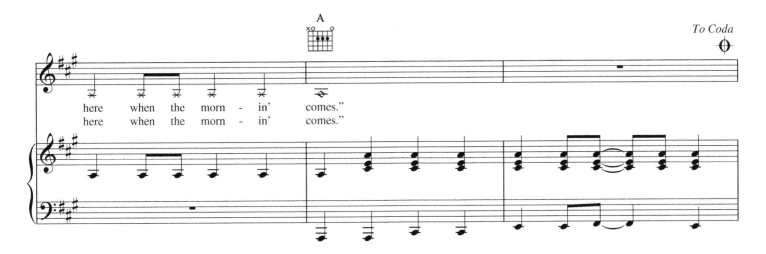

I bought this house so you know I'm boss.

Ain't no haint __ gon - na run me

off." In my kitch - en my

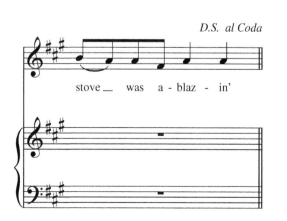

stove __ was a - blaz - in'

Say, "Yes, __ I'll be here when the morn - in'

Highway to Hell

Words and Music by Angus Young,
Malcolm Young and Bon Scott

Liv - in' eas - y,
No _____ stop signs,

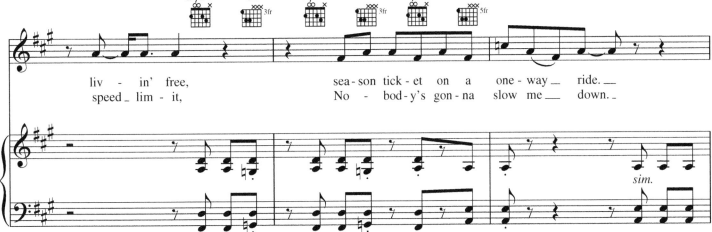

liv - in' free,
speed _ lim - it,

sea - son tick - et on a one - way _ ride. _
No - bod - y's gon - na slow me _ down. _

sim.

Ask - in' noth - in',   leave _ me be,   tak - in' ev - 'ry - thin' _
Like _ a wheel,   gon - na spin it.   No - bod - y's gon - na

in my stride. _   Don't _ need rea - son,   don't _ need rhyme,
mess me a - round. _   Hey, _ Sa - tan,   payin' _ my dues,

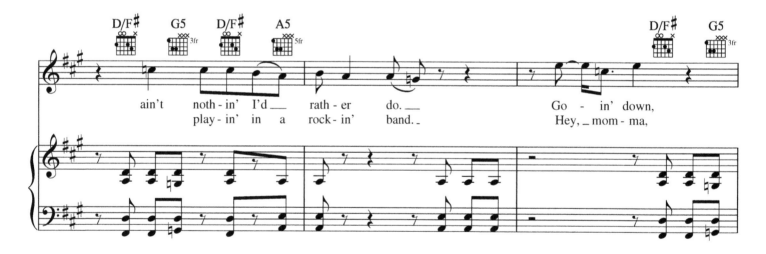

ain't noth - in' I'd _ rath - er do. _   Go - in' down,
play - in' in a rock - in' band. _   Hey, _ mom - ma,

par - ty time, _   my friends are gon - na be there, too. _
look at me, _   I'm on my way to the prom - ised land. _

I'm on the high - way to hell, ___ on the
I'm on the high - way to hell, ___

high - way to hell. ___ high - way to hell, _
high - way to hell. ___ I'm on the high - way to hell, _

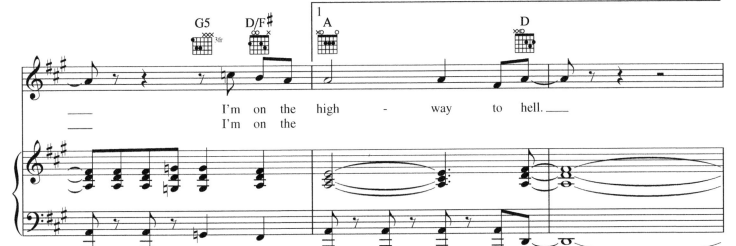

___ I'm on the high - way to hell. ___
I'm on the

high - way to hell, _____ mmm.

Don't stop me! _____

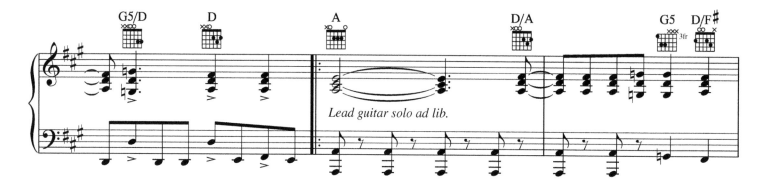

Lead guitar solo ad lib.

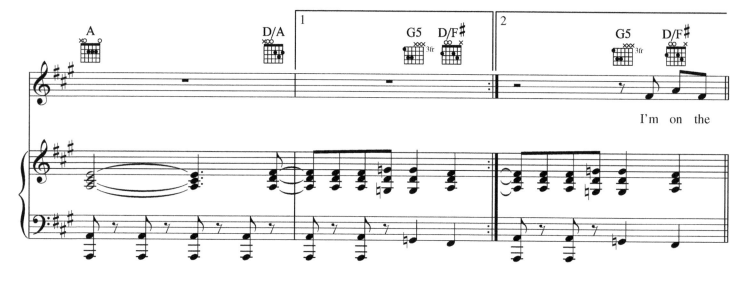

I'm on the

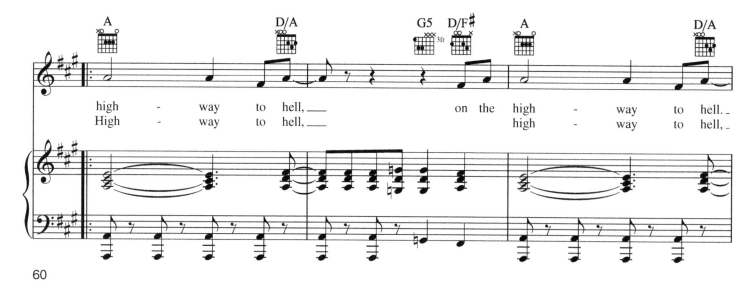

high - way to hell, _____   on the high - way to hell.
High - way to hell, _____   high - way to hell,

I'm on the high - way to hell, ___ on the
high - way to hell, ___

high - way to...

high - way to...

Very slowly and freely

And I'm go - in' down ___ all the way, ___ wow! ___

on the high - way to hell.

Little Shop of Horrors

from the Stage Production LITTLE SHOP OF HORRORS

Words by Howard Ashman
Music by Alan Menken

Medium Rock 'n' Roll beat

Lit - tle shop, __ lit - tle shop-pa hor - rors. Lit - tle shop, __ lit - tle shop-pa ter - ror. Call a cop. __ Lit - tle shop-pa hor - rors.

No, oh, oh, no - oh! _____ Lit - tle shop, __ lit -

- tle shop-pa hor - rors. Bop - sh' - bop, __ lit - tle shop-pa ter - ror.

Watch 'em drop. __ Lit - tle shop-pa hor-rors. No, oh, oh, no - oh! __

Shing - a - ling, what a creep-y thing to be hap - pen - ing! __ (Look

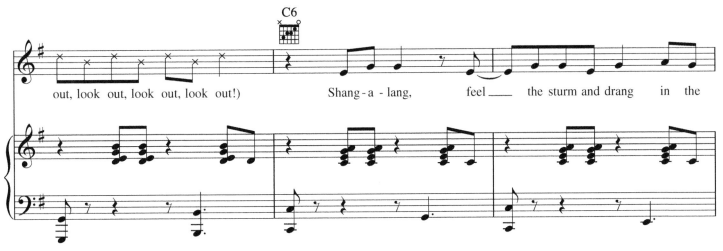

out, look out, look out, look out!) Shang - a - lang, feel __ the sturm and drang in the

63

air. _____ (Yeah, _ yeah, _ yeah.) _____ Sha - la - la,

stop right where you are. Don't move a thing. __ You bet - ter,

you bet - ter, tell - in' you you bet - ter tell your ma - ma

some-thin's gon - na get her. She bet - ter, ev - 'ry - bod - y bet - ter be - ware. _

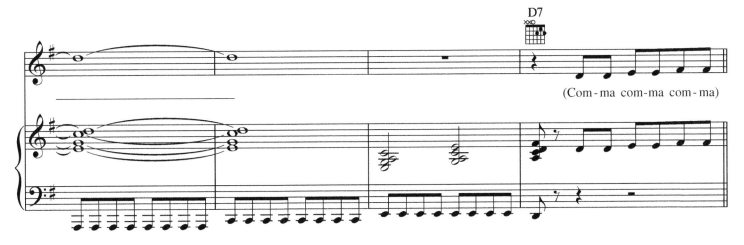

(Com-ma com-ma com-ma)

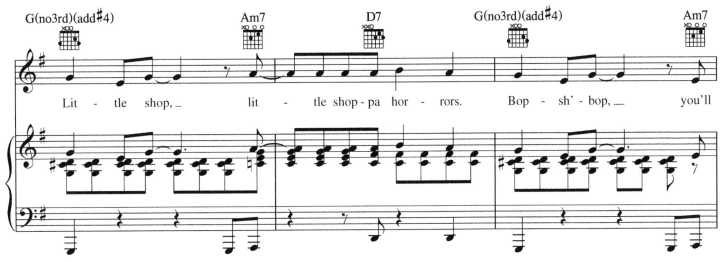

Lit — tle shop, __ lit — tle shop-pa hor - rors. Bop sh' - bop, __ you'll

nev - er stop the ter - ror. Lit — tle shop, __ lit — tle shop-pa hor - rors.

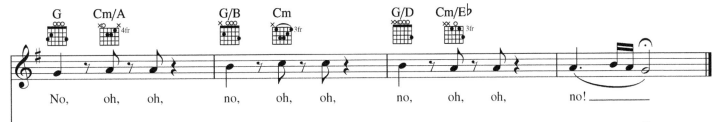

No, oh, oh, no, oh, oh, no, oh, oh, no! _____

Monster Mash

Words and Music by
Bobby Pickett and Leonard Capizzi

1. (Spoken:) I was working in the lab late one night, when my eyes beheld
2.-5. (See additional lyrics)

an eerie sight, for my monster from his slab began to rise, and

zombies were having fun.   The party had just

begun.   The guests included Wolfman,

Dracula and his son.   3. The monster mash.

Mash good.

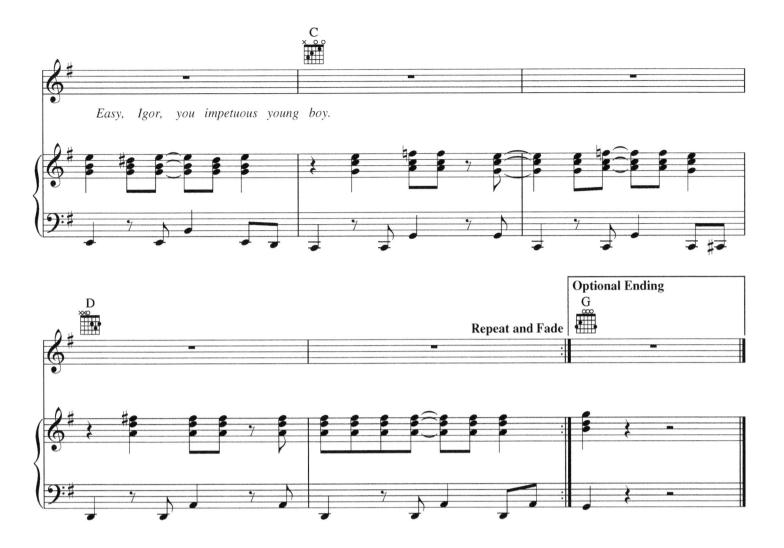

Easy, Igor, you impetuous young boy.

Additional Lyrics

2. *From my laboratory in the castle east,*
   To the master bedroom where the vampires feast,
   The ghouls all came from their humble abodes
   To get a jolt from my electrodes.
   (*to Chorus:* They did the mash)

3. *The scene was rockin'. All were digging the sounds.*
   Igor on chains, backed by his baying hounds.
   The coffin-bangers were about to arrive
   With their vocal group, "The Crypt-Kicker Five."
   (*to Chorus:* They played the mash)

4. *Out from his coffin, Drac's voice did ring.*
   Seems he was troubled by just one thing.
   He opened the lid and shook his fist,
   And said, "Whatever happened to my Transylvanian Twist?"
   (*to Chorus:* It's now the mash)

5. *Now everything's cool, Drac's a part of the band.*
   And my monster mash is the hit of the land.
   For you, the living, this mash was meant, too,
   When you get to my door, tell them Boris sent you.
   (*to Chorus:* Then you can mash)

The Mummy

from THE MUMMY

By Jerry Goldsmith

Moderately

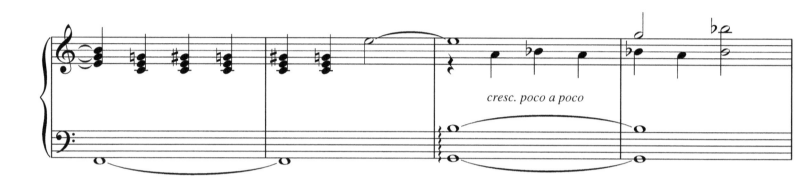

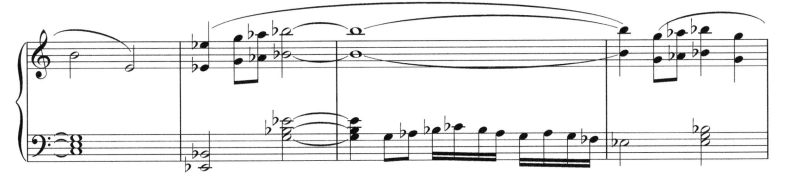

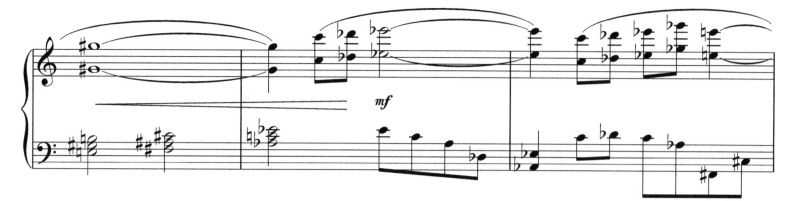

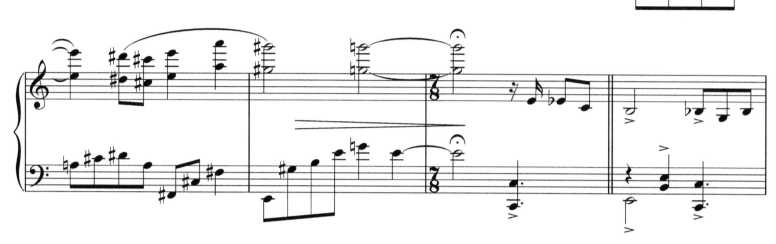

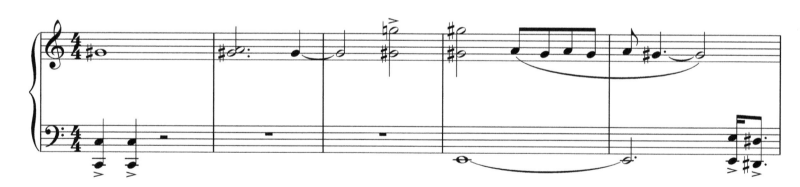

73

The Munsters Theme

from the Television Series

By Jack Marshall

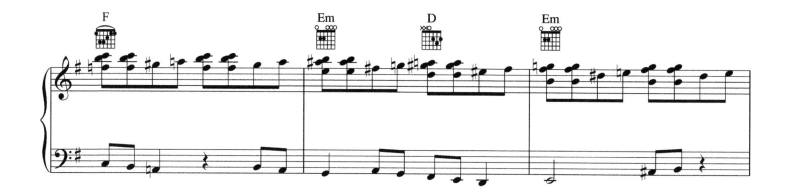

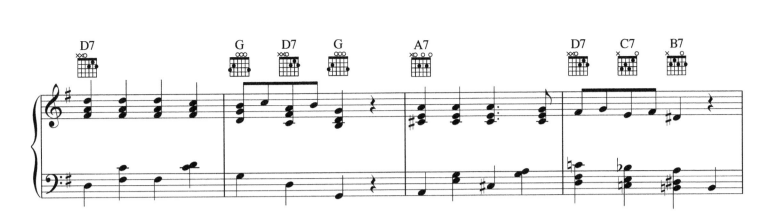

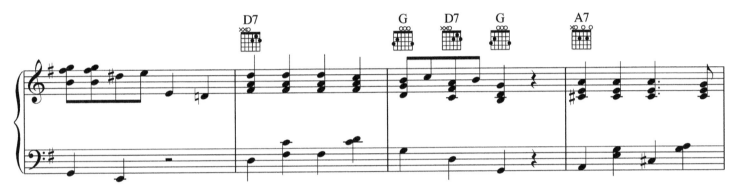

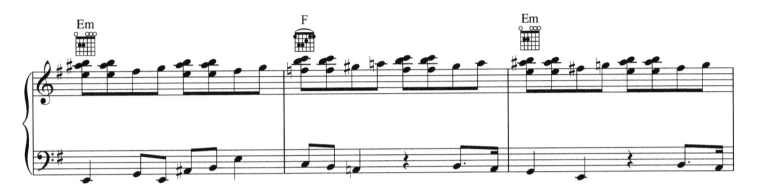

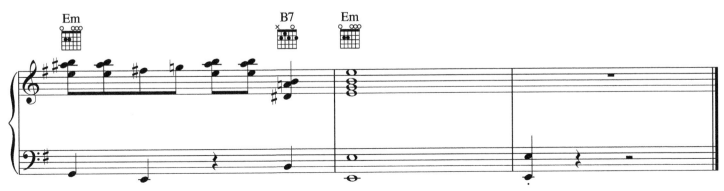

The Phantom of the Opera

from THE PHANTOM OF THE OPERA

Lyrics by
Charles Hart
Additional Lyrics by
Richard Stilgoe and Mike Batt

Music by
Andrew Lloyd Webber

Allegro vivace

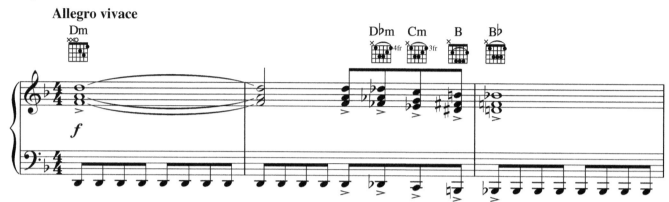

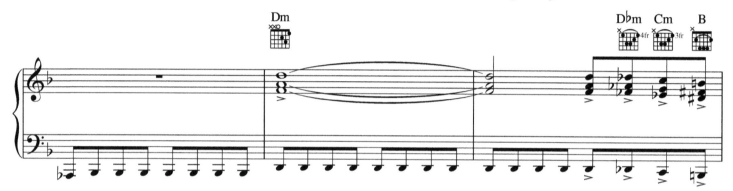

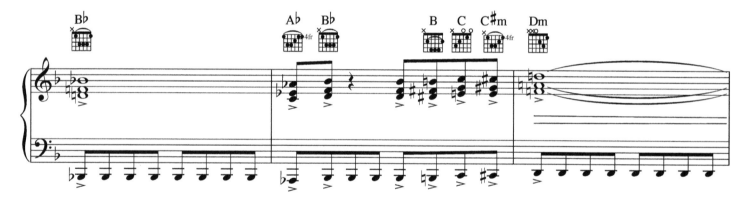

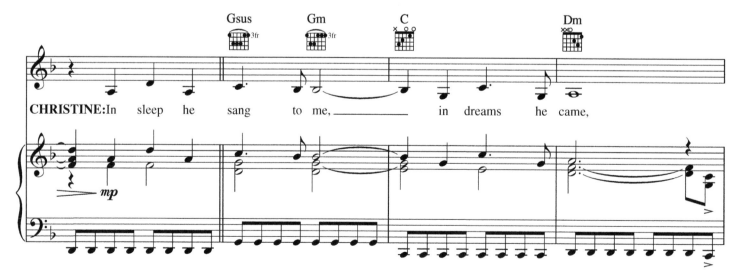

CHRISTINE: In sleep he sang to me, _____ in dreams he came,

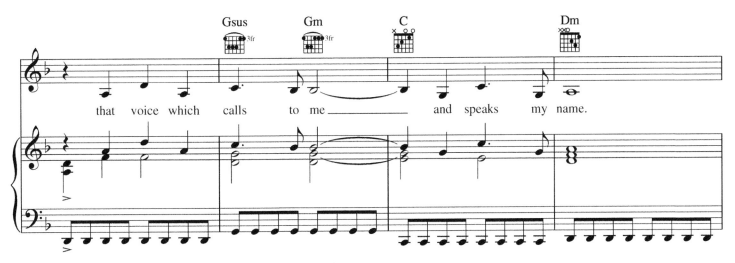

that voice which calls to me _____ and speaks my name.

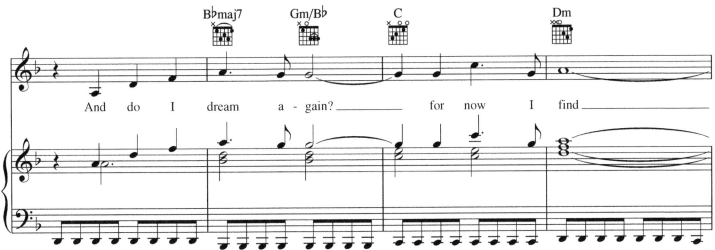

And do I dream a - gain? _____ for now I find _____

_____ the phan - tom of the op - er - a is

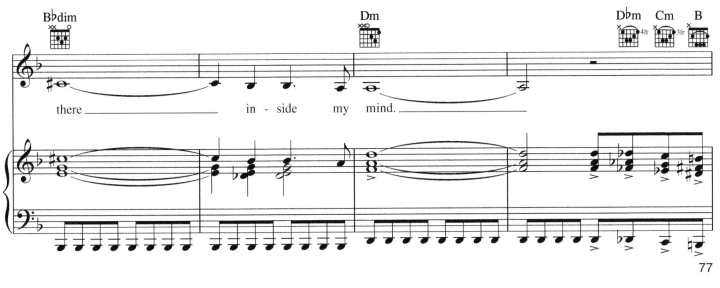

there _____ in - side my mind. _____

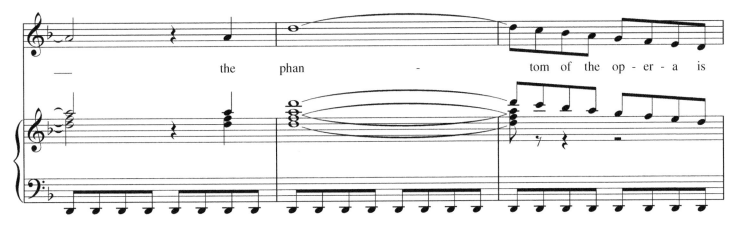

77

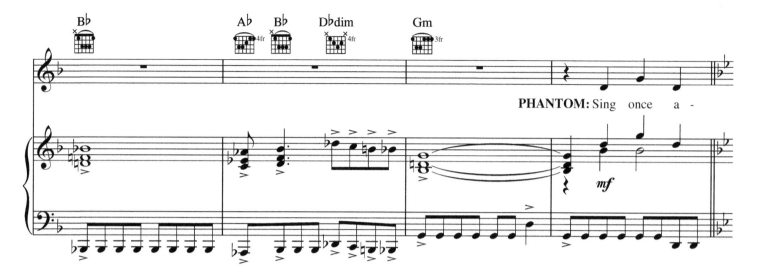

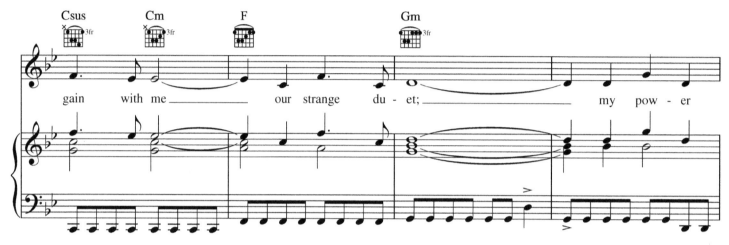

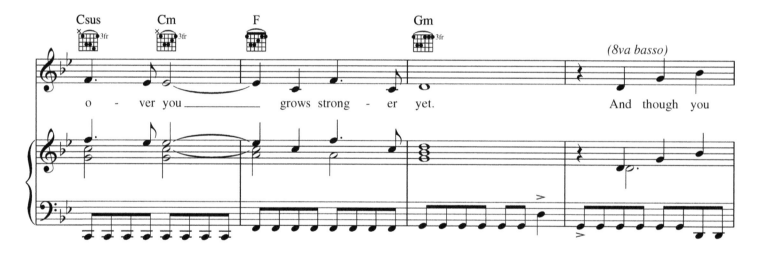

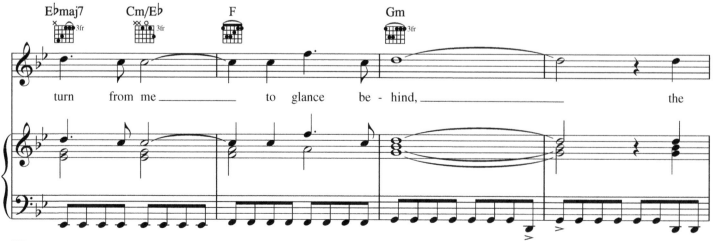

78

phan - tom of the op-er-a is there _____ in - side your

mind. _____

CHRISTINE: Those who have seen your face _____ draw back in

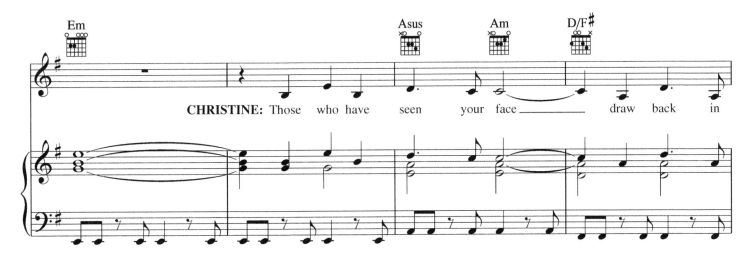

fear. _____ I am the mask you wear, _____ it's me they PHANTOM:

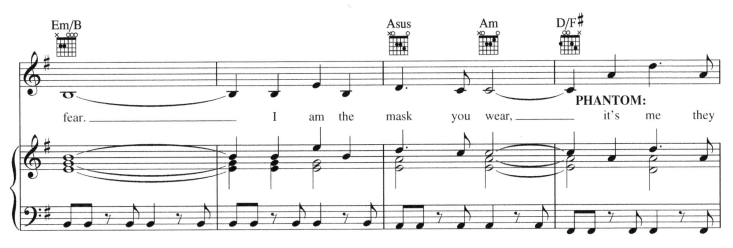

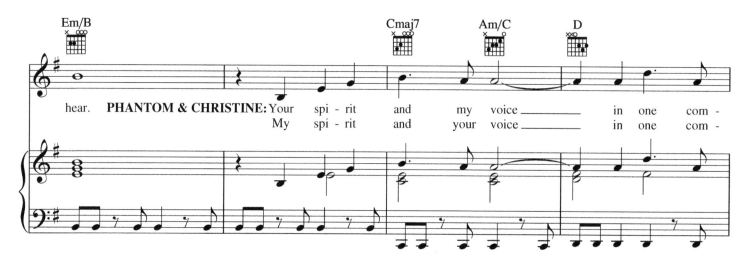

hear. **PHANTOM & CHRISTINE:** Your spi - rit and my voice _____ in one com -
My spi - rit and your voice _____ in one com -

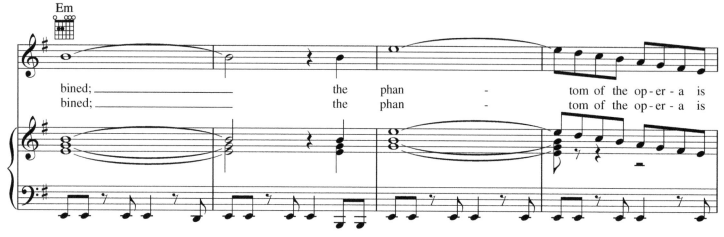

bined; _____ the phan - tom of the op - er - a is
bined; _____ the phan - tom of the op - er - a is

VOICES:

He's there, *the phan - tom of the*
there in - side my mind.
there in - side your mind.

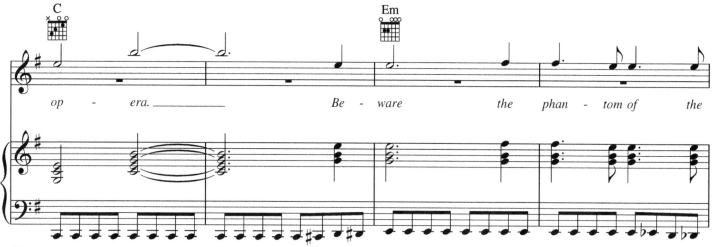

op - era. _____ *Be - ware* *the phan - tom of the*

op - era. _____

In all your

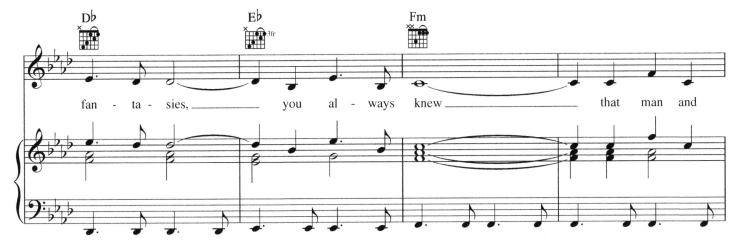

fan - ta - sies, _____ you al - ways knew _____ that man and

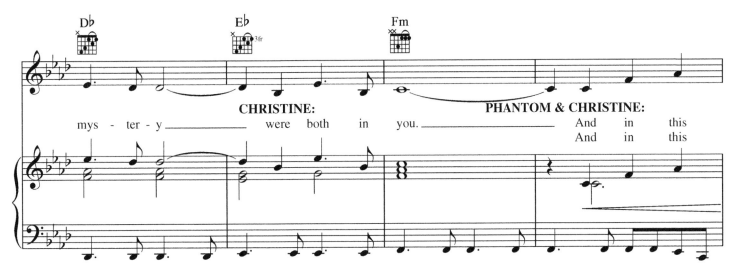

CHRISTINE:

mys - ter - y _____ were both in you. _____

PHANTOM & CHRISTINE:
And in this
And in this

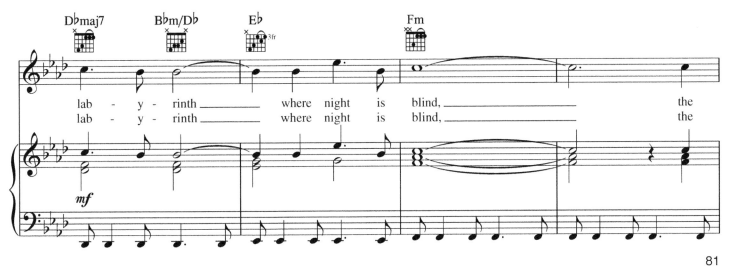

lab - y - rinth _____ where night is blind, _____ the
lab - y - rinth _____ where night is blind, _____ the

phan - tom of the op-er-a is there _____ in - side my
phan - tom of the op-er-a is there _____ in - side your

mind.
mind.

PHANTOM:
(Spoken:)Sing, my angel of music!

CHRISTINE: He's

there the phan - tom of the op - era. _____

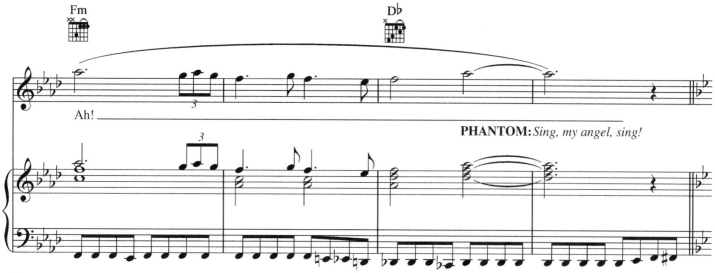

Ah! _____

PHANTOM: *Sing, my angel, sing!*

CHRISTINE: Ah!

PHANTOM: *(1st time only) Sing for me!*

CHRISTINE: Ah!

PHANTOM: *Sing, my*

angel of music!

CHRISTINE: Ah!

Ah!

Ah!

Psycho
(Prelude)
Theme from the Paramount Picture PSYCHO

Music by
Bernard Herrmann

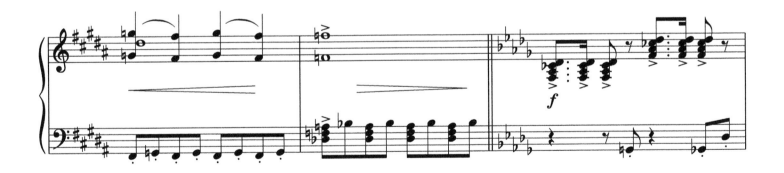

85

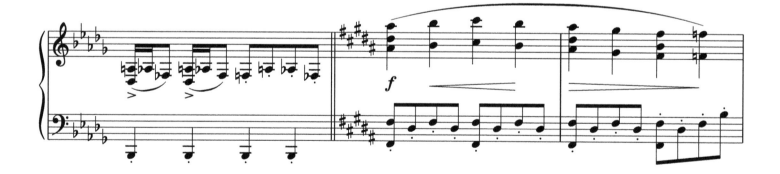

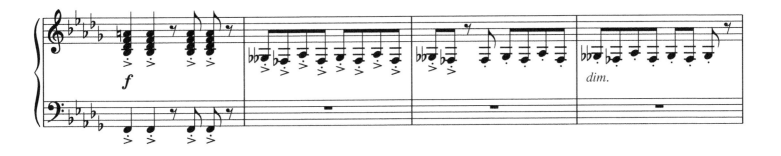

Purple People Eater

Words and Music by
Sheb Wooley

Additional Lyrics

3. I said, "Mister purple people eater, what's your line?"
   He said, "Eatin' purple people, and it sure is fine,
   But that's not the reason that I came to land,
   I wanna get a job in a rock and roll band."
   Chorus

4. And then he swung from the tree and he lit on the ground,
   And he started to rock, a-really rockin' around.
   It was a crazy ditty with a swingin' tune,
   Singa bop bapa loop a lap a loom bam boom.
   Chorus

5. Well, he went on his way and then what-a you know,
   I saw him last night on a TV show,
   He was blowin' it out, really knockin' 'em dead,
   Playin' rock 'n' roll music thru the horn in his head.
   Chorus

Silence of the Lambs
Theme from the Motion Picture SILENCE OF THE LAMBS

Music by
Howard Shore

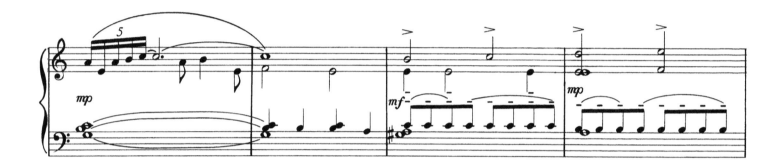

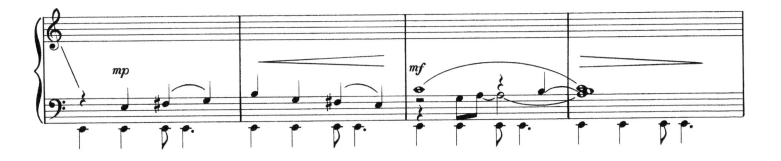

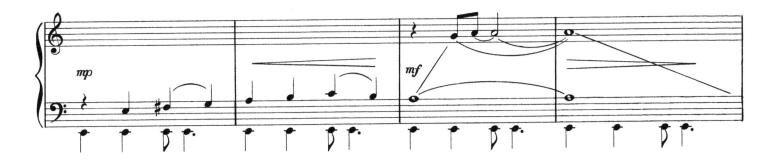

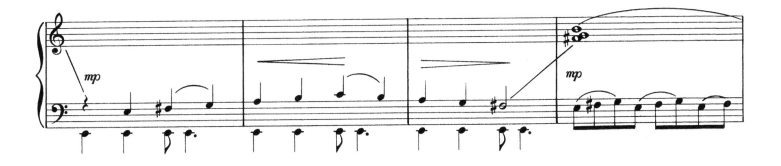

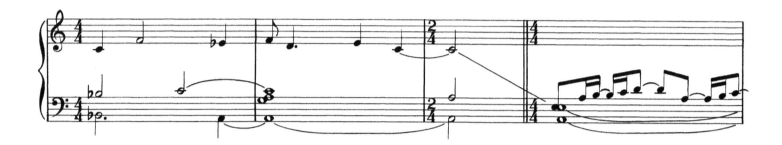

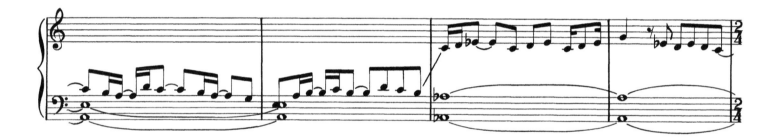

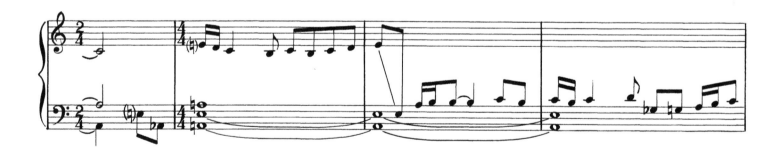

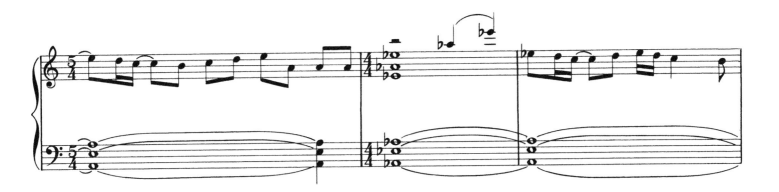

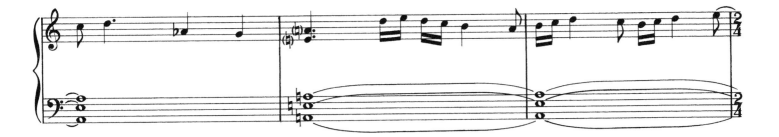

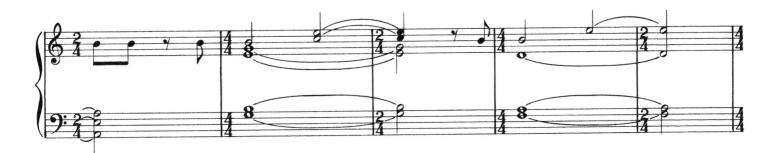

The Simpsons™ Halloween Special
Main Title Theme

from the Twentieth Century Fox Television Series THE SIMPSONS

By Danny Elfman

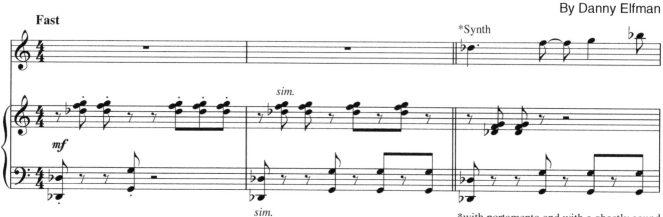

*with portamento and with a ghostly sound

The Sorcerer's Apprentice

By Paul Dukas

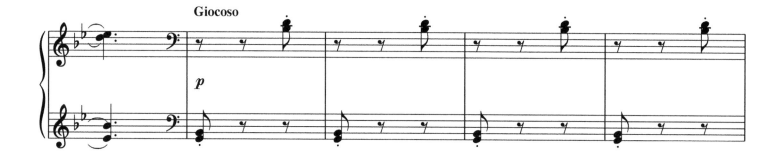

poco cresc.

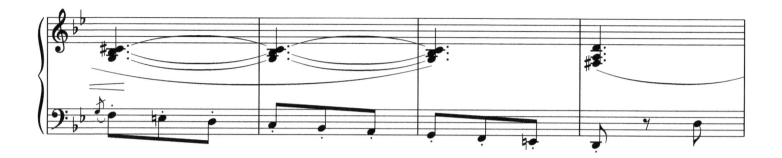

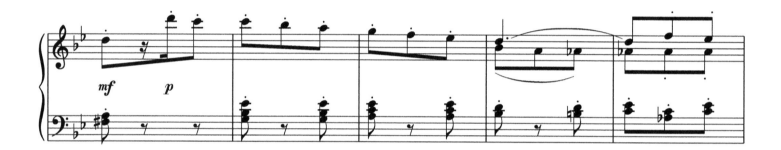

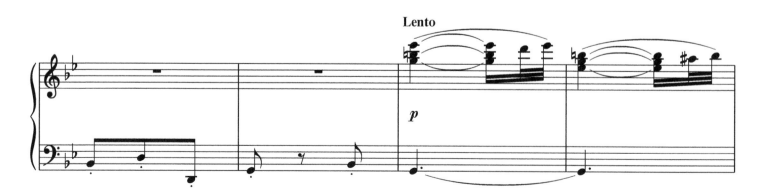

dolce espress.

dolce espress.

pp

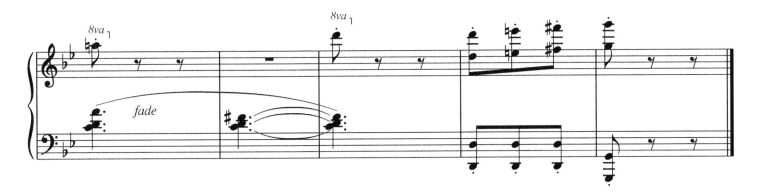

fade

Spooky

Words and Music by J.R. Cobb,
Buddy Buie, Harry Middlebrooks
and Mike Shapiro

In the cool of the ev-'ning as ev — 'ry-thing is get-tin' kind of

groo-vy, ___ I call you up and ask you if you'd

like to go with me and see a mo - vie.____ And

first you say no___you've got some plans for to-night, and then you stop and say

all right. Love is kind a craz-y with a spook-y lit-tle girl like you.____

You al-ways keep me guess-ing, I nev - er seem to know what you are

think - ing, And if a fel - ler looks at you, it's for

sure your lit - tle eye will be a - wink-ing.

I get con - fused___ 'cause I don't know where I stand___ and then you

smile and hold my hand, love is kind a craz-y with a

spook-y lit-tle girl like you, a spook-y.

If you de-cide___ you'd bet-ter stop this lit-tle game that you are

play-ing,___ I'm gon-na tell you all the things my

heart's been a-dy-ing to be say-ing.___ A-

just like a ghost,___ you've been haunt-ing my dreams,___ so I'll pro-

pose on hal-low-een. Love is kind-a craz-y with a

spook-y lit-tle girl like you. Spook-y.

Repeat and fade

Tales from the Crypt Theme

By Danny Elfman

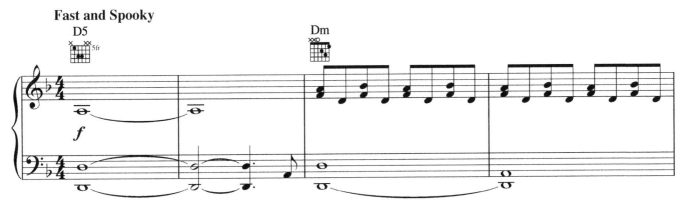

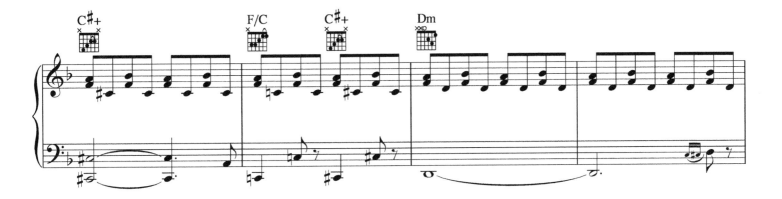

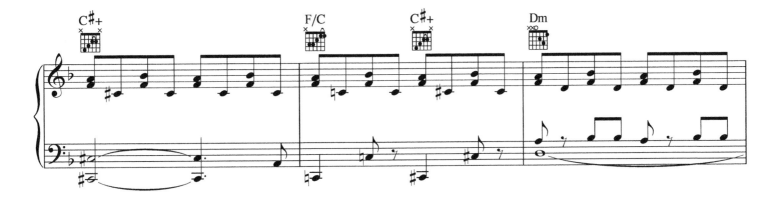

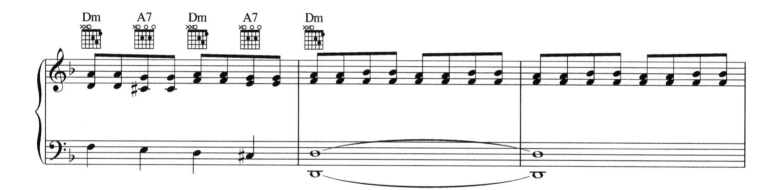

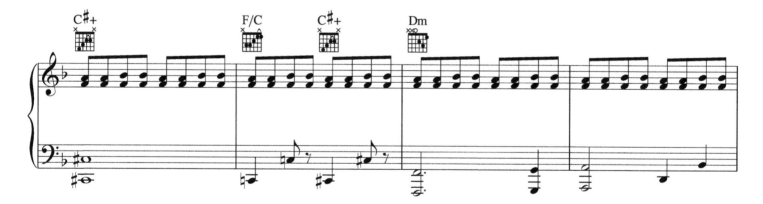

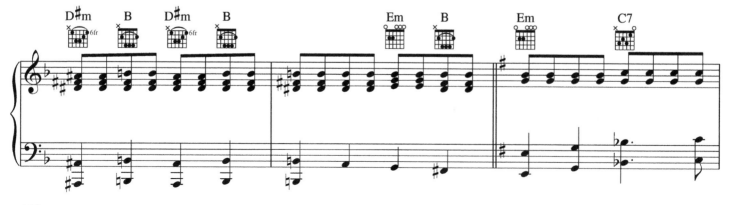

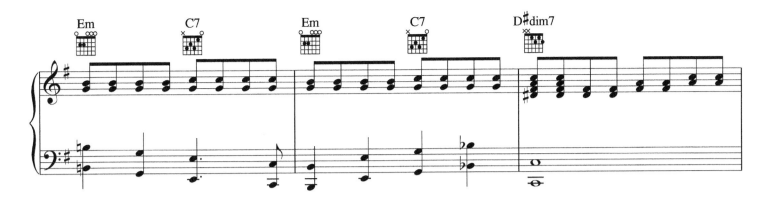

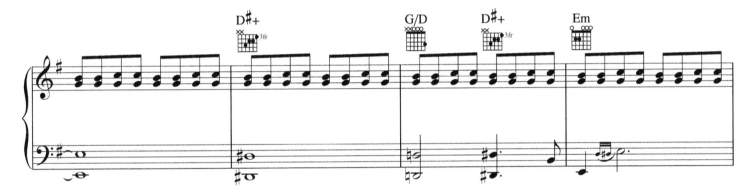

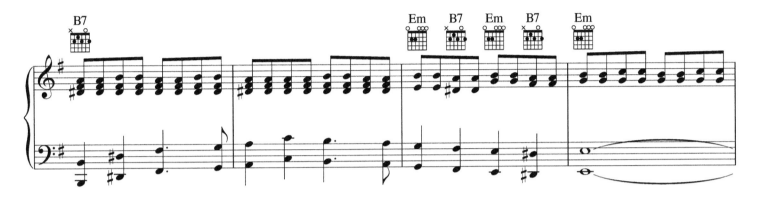

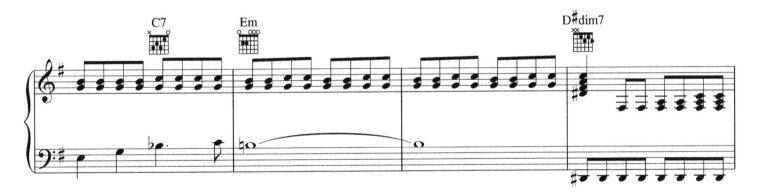

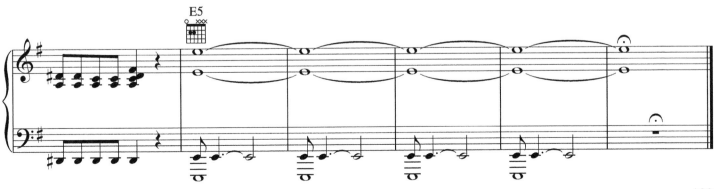

The Thing

Words and Music by
Charles R. Grean

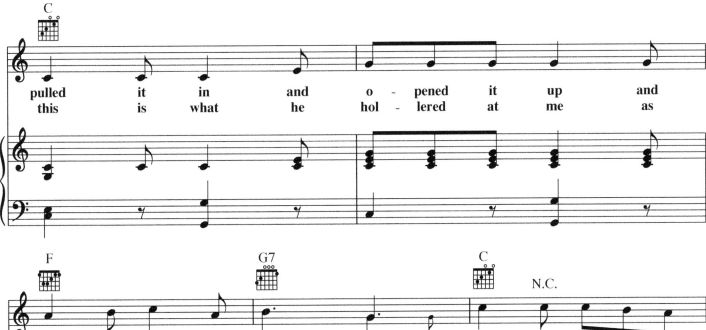

pulled   it   in   and   o - pened   it   up   and
this   is   what   he   hol - lered   at   me   as

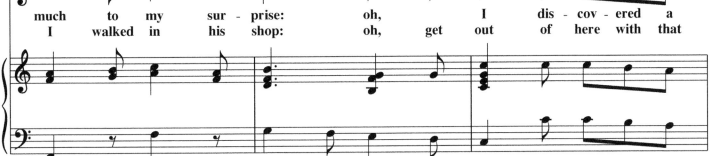

much   to   my   sur - prise: oh,   I   dis - cov - ered   a
I   walked   in   his   shop: oh,   get   out   of   here   with   that

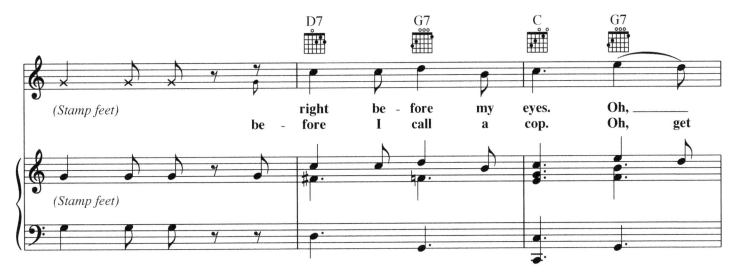

(Stamp feet)   right   be - fore   my   eyes.   Oh, _____
              be - fore   I   call   a   cop.   Oh,   get

(Stamp feet)

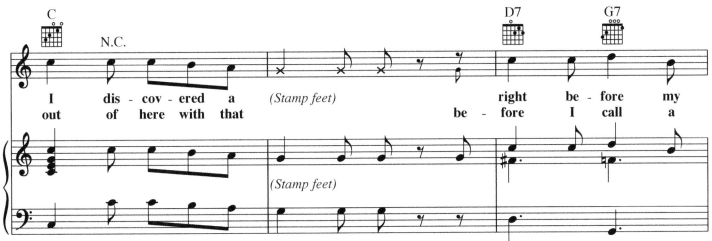

I   dis - cov - ered   a   *(Stamp feet)*   right be - fore   my
out   of   here   with   that   be - fore   I   call   a

(Stamp feet)

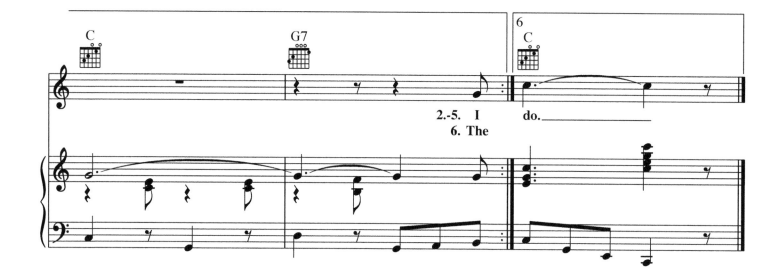

Additional Lyrics

3. I turned around and got right out a-runnin' for my life,
   And then I took it home with me to give it to my wife.
   But this is what she hollered at me as I walked in the door:
   Oh, get out of here with that xxx and don't come back no more.
   Oh, get out of here with that xxx and don't come back no more.

4. I wandered all around the town until I chanced to meet
   A hobo who was looking for handout on the street.
   He said he'd take most any old thing, he was a desperate man,
   But when I showed him the xxx, he turned around and ran.
   Oh, when I showed him the xxx, he turned around and ran.

5. I wandered on for many years, a victim of my fate,
   Until one day I came upon Saint Peter at the gate.
   And when I tried to take it inside he told me where to go:
   Get out of here with that xxx and take it down below.
   Oh, get out of here with that xxx and take it down below.

6. The moral of the story is if you're out on the beach
   And you should see a great big box and it's within your reach,
   Don't ever stop and open it up, that's my advice to you,
   'Cause you'll never get rid of the xxx, no matter what you do.
   Oh, you'll never get rid of the xxx, no matter what you do.

This Is Halloween

from Tim Burton's THE NIGHTMARE BEFORE CHRISTMAS

Music and Lyrics by
Danny Elfman

Shadow:
Boys and girls of ev-er-y age, wouldn't you like to see some-thing strange?

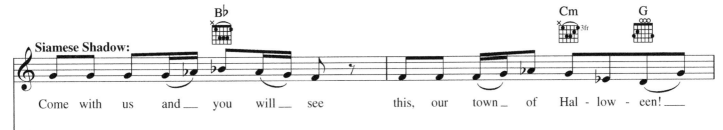

Siamese Shadow:
Come with us and __ you will __ see this, our town __ of Hal-low-een! __

115

Ev-'ry-bod-y's wait-ing for the next sur-prise. 'Round that cor-ner, man, hid-ing in the trash - can,

Corpse Chorus:

some thing's wait-ing now to pounce, and how you'll scream! This is Hal-low een, red and black and slim - y green.

Harlequin Demon, Werewolf, Melting Man:

Werewolf: **Witches:**

Aren't you scared? Well, that's just fine! Say it once, say it twice, take a chance and roll the dice.

Ride with the moon in the dead of night. Ev - 'ry - bod - y scream, ev - 'ry - bod - y scream

Hanging Tree:

dim.

f

116

Bm　　Gm

Hal-low-een! Hal-low-een! Hal-low-een! Hal-low-een! Hal-low-een! Hal-low-een!

p

C#m　　G#7/C#　　　C#m

Child Corpse Trio:

Ten - der lump - lings ev - er - y - where. Life's no fun with - out a good scare.

f

B　　　　C#m　G#7

Parent Corpses:

That's our job, but we're not___ mean in our town___ of Hal - low - een.___

G#m　E　G#m　　Bm　　C#7　F#m

Corpse Chorus:　**Mayor:**　**Mayor, Corpse Chorus:**

In this town, don't we love it now? Ev - 'ry-one's wait-ing for the next sur - prise.

heavily

118

119

120

Thriller

Words and Music by
Rod Temperton

Moderately bright

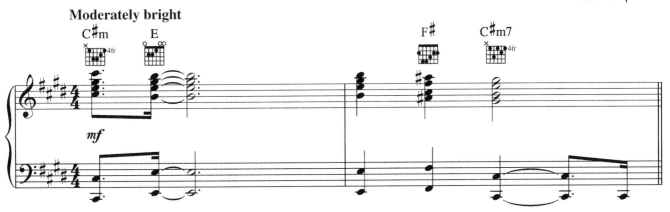

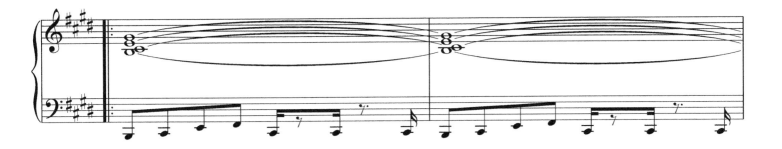

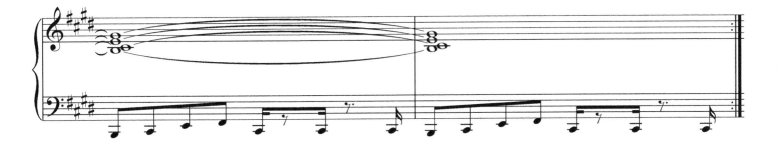

It's   close   to mid -   night,____   and
You   hear   the   door ____   slam ____   and
They're   out   to   get ____   you. ____   There's

121

some-thin' e - vil's lurk - in' in the dark.
re - al - ize there's no - where left to run.
de - mons clos - in' on ev - 'ry side.

Un - der the moon - light _____ you
You feel the cold __ hand, _____ and
They will pos - sess __ you _____ un -

see a sight that al - most stops your heart. _____ You try to scream, __
won - der if you'll ev - er see the sun. _____ You close your eyes, __
less you change that num - ber on your dial. _____ Now is the time __

122

but   ter - ror takes _ the sound _ be - fore _ you make _
and   hope that this __ is   just ___ i - mag - i - na -
for   you and I ___ to cud - dle close _ to - geth -

___ it. _____
- tion. _____
- er. _____

You   start to freeze _
But all the while, _
All through the night _

as   hor - ror looks _ you right _ be - tween _ the eyes. _
you   hear the crea - ture creep - in' up ___ be - hind. _
I'll   save you from _ the ter - ror on ___ the screen. _

You're par - a - lyzed. ____ 'Cause this is
You're out of time. ____ 'Cause this is
I'll make you see ____ that this is

thrill - er, ___ thrill - er night, and
thrill - er, ___ thrill - er night. There
thrill - er, ___ thrill - er night, 'cause

no one's gon - na save ___ you from the beast ___ a - bout to strike. You know, it's
ain't no sec - ond chance ___ a - gainst the thing ___ with for - ty eyes. ___ You know, it's
I can thrill you more ___ than an - y ghost ___ would dare to try. ___ Girl, this is

thrill - er, ___ thrill - er night. You're
thrill - er, ___ thrill - er night. You're
thrill - er, ___ thrill - er night, so

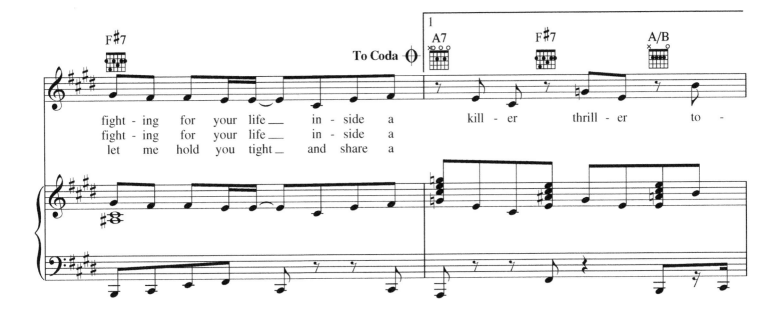

fight - ing for your life ___ in - side a kill - er thrill - er to -
fight - ing for your life ___ in - side a
let me hold you tight ___ and share a

To Coda ⊕

night. ___

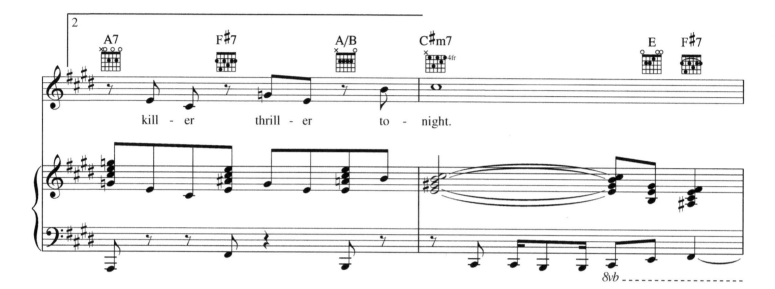

kill - er thrill - er to - night.

Night crea - tures call and __ the dead start __ to walk in __ their

mas - quer - ade.

There's __

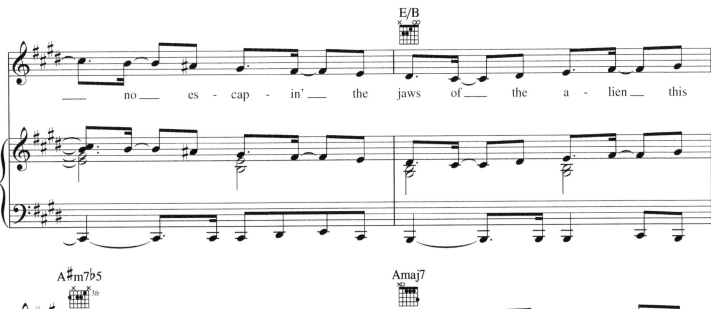

no es-cap-in' the jaws of the a-lien this

time. This is the end of your

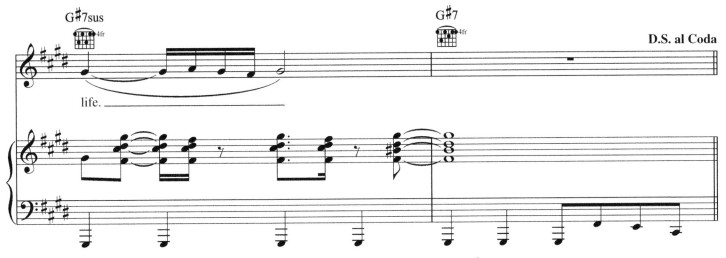

life.

D.S. al Coda

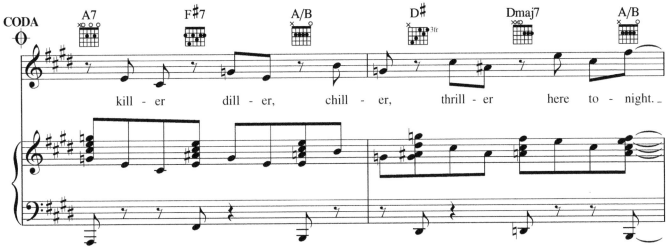

CODA

kill-er dill-er, chill-er, thrill-er here to-night.

'Cause this is thrill - er,

thrill - er night, girl, I can thrill you more __ than an - y ghost __

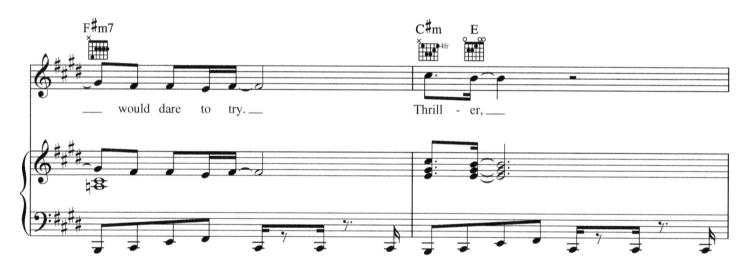

__ would dare to try. __ Thrill - er, __

thrill - er night, so let me hold you tight __ and share a

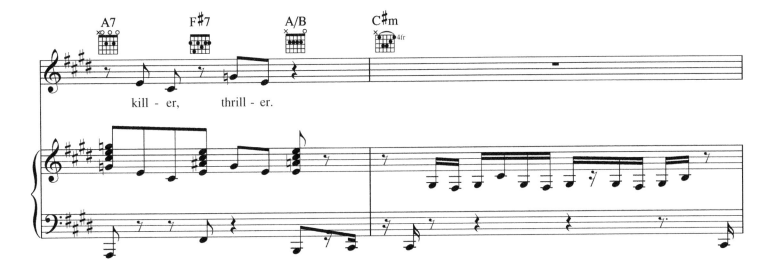

kill - er,   thrill - er.

I'm gon-na thrill you to - night. ____   1. *(See spoken lyrics)*

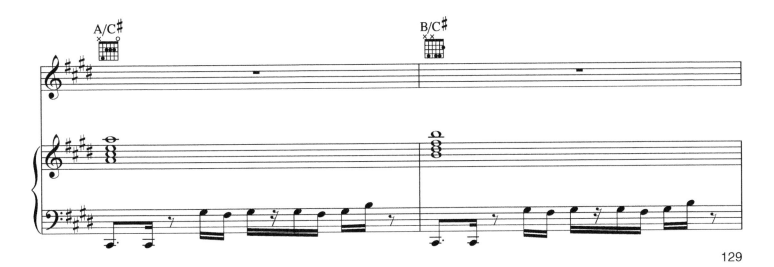

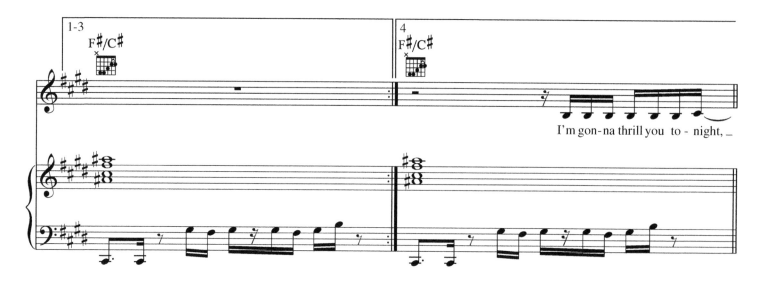

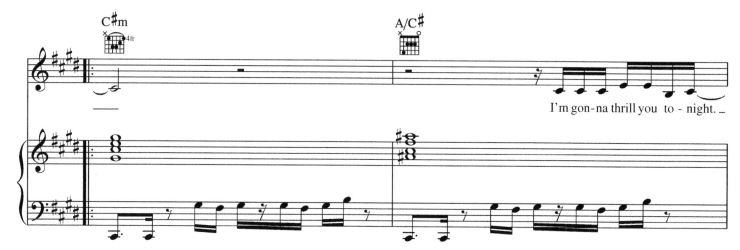

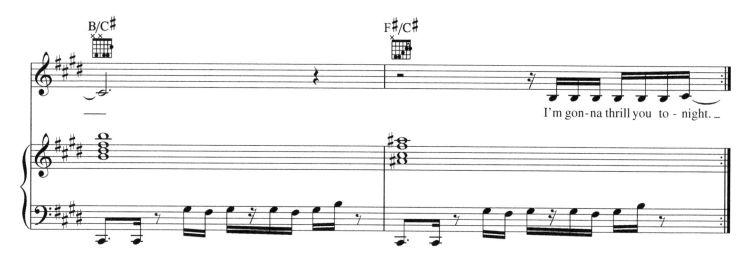

2. (See spoken lyrics)

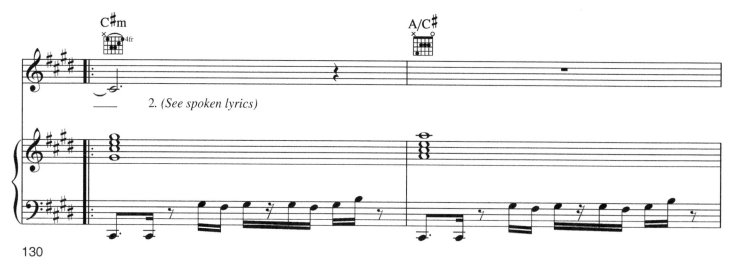

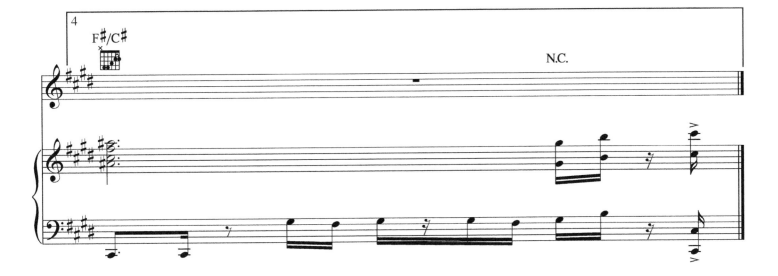

Spoken Lyrics

1. Darkness falls across the land.
   The midnight hour is close at hand.
   Creatures crawl in search of blood
   To terrorize y'all's neighborhood.
   And whosoever shall be found
   Without the soul for getting down
   Must stand and face the hounds of hell
   And rot inside a corpse's shell.

2. The foulest stench is in the air,
   The funk of forty thousand years,
   And grizzly ghouls from every tomb
   Are closing in to seal your doom.
   And though you fight to stay alive,
   Your body starts to shiver,
   For no mere mortal can resist
   The evil of a thriller.

Time Warp

from THE ROCKY HORROR PICTURE SHOW

Words and Music by
Richard O'Brien

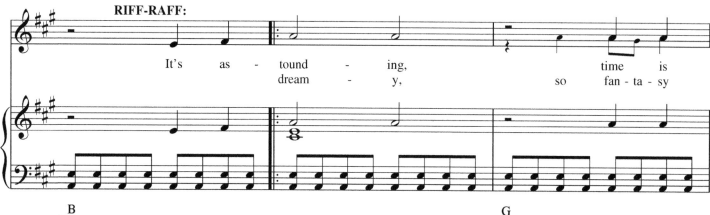

RIFF-RAFF:

It's as - tound - ing,   time is
dream - y,   so fan - ta - sy

fleet - ing, _____   mad - ness
free   me, _____   so you can't see me, _

takes its toll.
no, not at all.   Lis - ten
In an - oth - er di -

close - ly, / not for ver - y much long -
men - sion, / with voy - eur - is - tic in - ten -

er, / I've got to keep _____ con -
tion, / well se - clud - ed, I'll _____ see

trol. _____ I re - mem - ber _____
all. _____ With a bit of a mind flip _____

do - ing the Time Warp, _____
you're in - to the time slip. _____

133

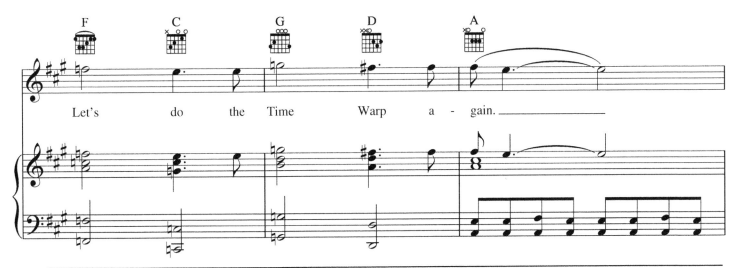

Let's do the Time Warp a - gain.

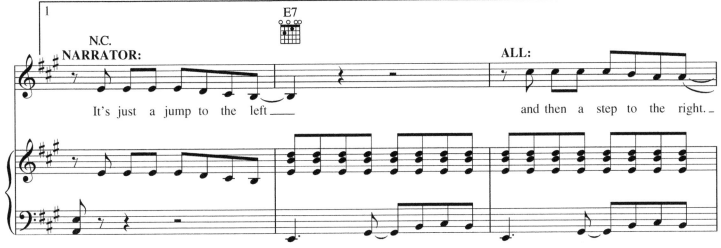

1

NARRATOR: It's just a jump to the left ___

ALL: and then a step to the right. ___

___ **NARRATOR:** With your hands on your hips, ___

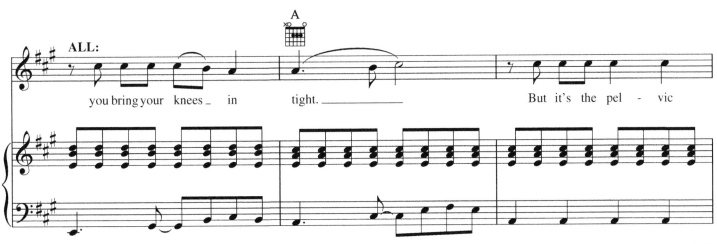

ALL: you bring your knees ___ in tight. ___ But it's the pel - vic

thrusts, _____ that real - ly drive you in - sane. _____

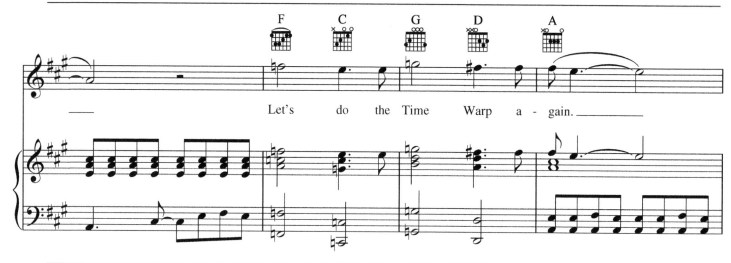

____ Let's do the Time Warp a - gain. _____

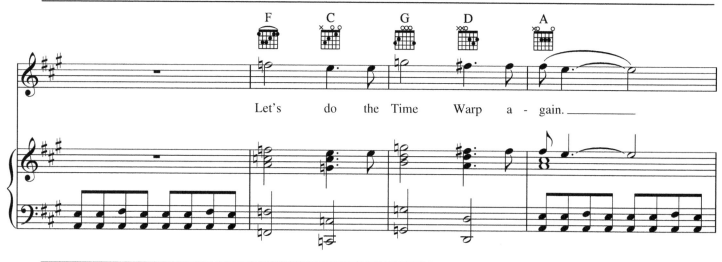

Let's do the Time Warp a - gain. _____

MAGENTA:

COLUMBIA:

It's so   Well, I was tap - ping down the street, just - a

136

hav-ing a think,__ when a snake of a guy__ gave me an e-vil wink.__ It

D   A

shook me up,__ it took me by sur-prise, had a pick-up truck__ and the

E   D

dev-il's eyes.__   He stared at me,__ and I felt a change.__

A   F   C

                                                    ALL:

Time meant noth-ing; nev-er would a - gain.__   Let's do the

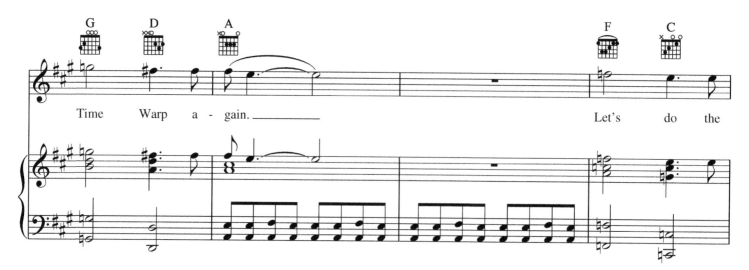

Time Warp a - gain._____ Let's do the

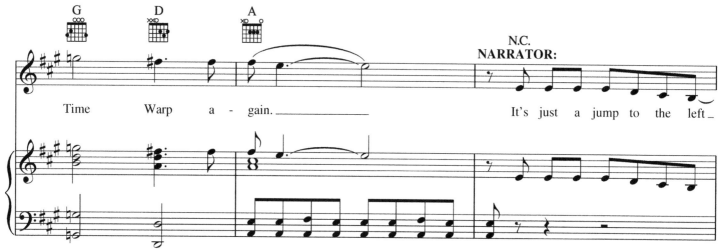

Time Warp a - gain._____

N.C.
NARRATOR:
It's just a jump to the left _

ALL:
and then a step to the right. _____

N.C.
NARRATOR:
With your hands on your hips, ___

ALL:
you bring your knees _ in

tight. _____ But it's the pel - vic thrusts, _____

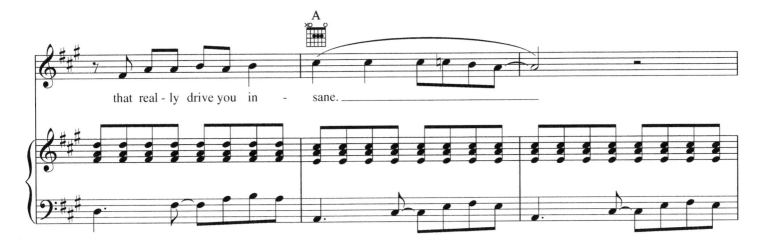

that real - ly drive you in - sane. _____

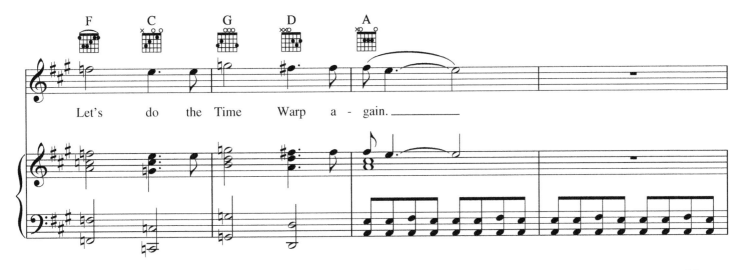

Let's do the Time Warp a - gain. _____

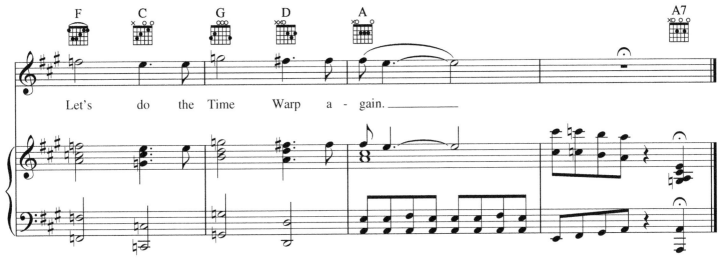

Let's do the Time Warp a - gain. _____

Toccata and Fugue in D Minor

By Johann Sebastian Bach

Adagio

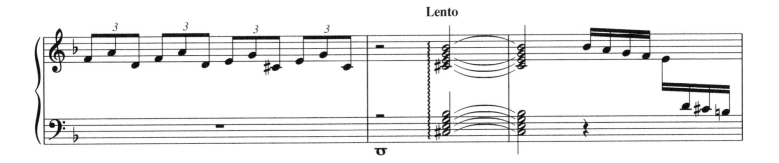

Prestissimo

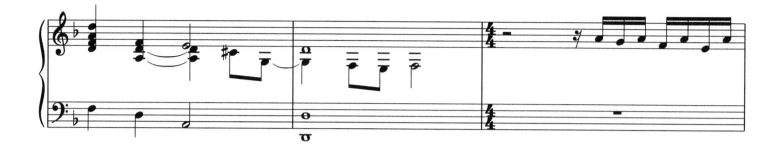

Recitativo

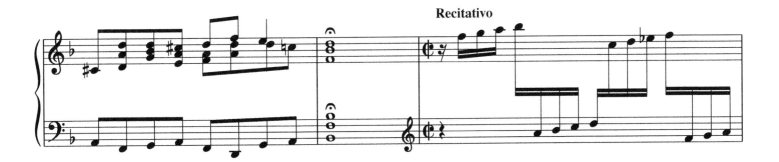

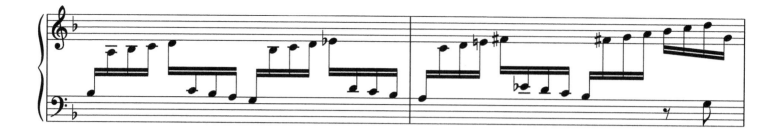

Adagissimo

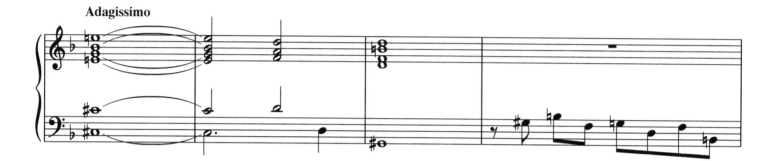

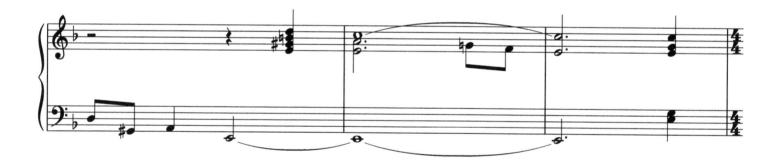

Vivace

Molto Adagio

Tubular Bells
Theme from THE EXORCIST

By Mike Oldfield

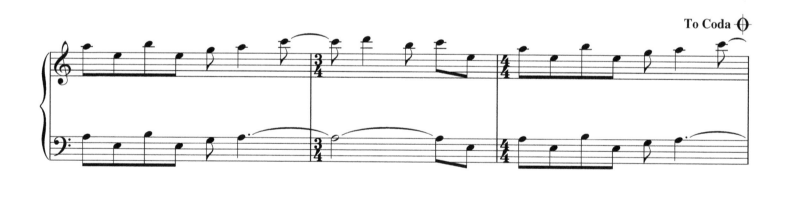

To Coda ⊕

D.S. al Coda

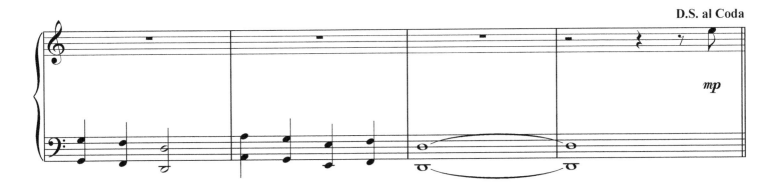

mp

CODA

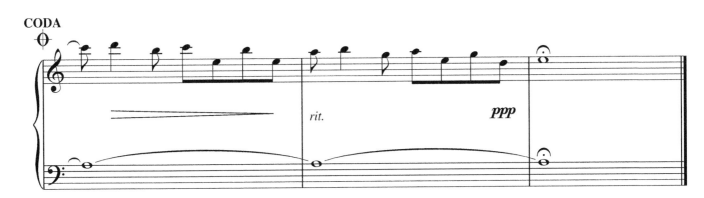

rit.

ppp

Twilight Zone Main Title

from the Television Series

By Maurius Constant

Welcome to My Nightmare

Words and Music by
Alice Cooper and Richard Wagner

you be - long.___
when we come down.___
you be - long.___

A noc - tur - nal va - ca -
We sweat and laugh and scream___
We sweat and laugh and scream___

tion,
___ here,
___ here,

un - nec - es - sar - y se - da - tion;
'cause life is just a dream___ here;
'cause life is just a dream___ here;

you want to feel at home___ 'cause you be - long.
you know in - side you feel___ right at home ___ here.___
you know in - side you feel___ right at home ___ here.___

B7+9

Wel - come to my night - mare, woah.___
Wel - come to my break - down, woah.___
Wel - come to my night - mare, woah.___

You're wel-come to my night - mare, yeah.

Wel - come to my break - down.

Tacet

Repeat and fade

Repeat and fade

Werewolves of London

Words and Music by Warren Zevon,
Robert Wachtel and LeRoy Marinel

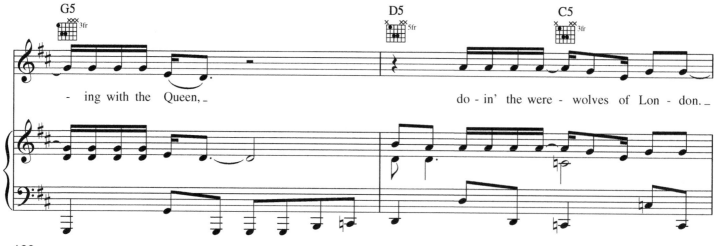

Theme from The X-Files

from the Twentieth Century Fox Television Series THE X-FILES

By Mark Snow

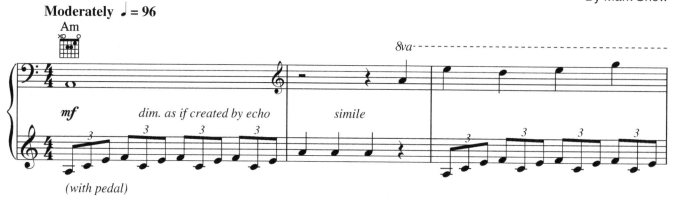

(with pedal)

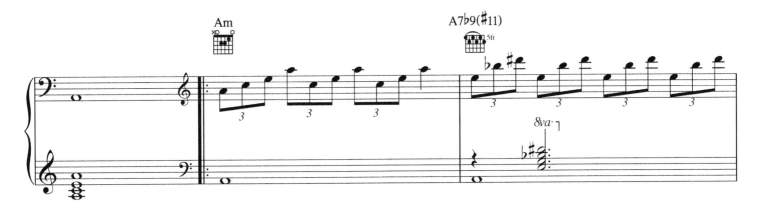

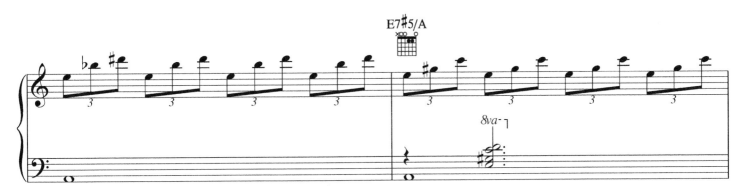

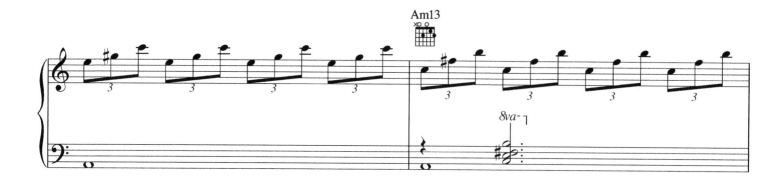

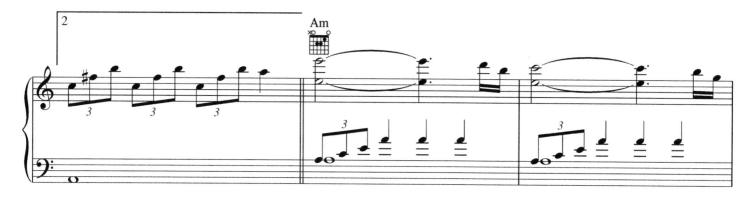

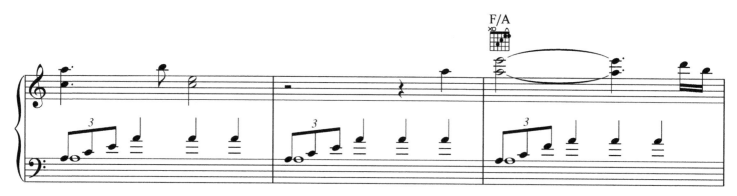

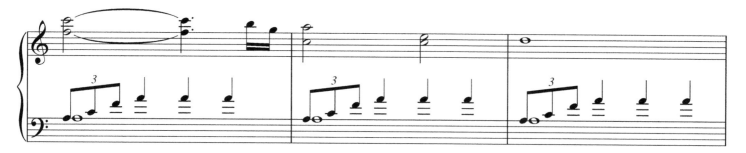

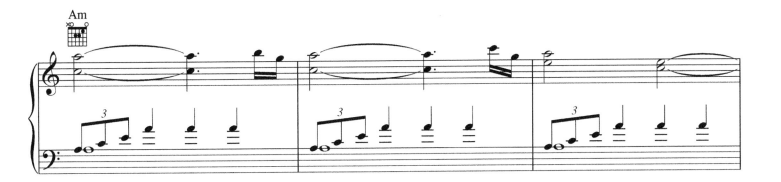

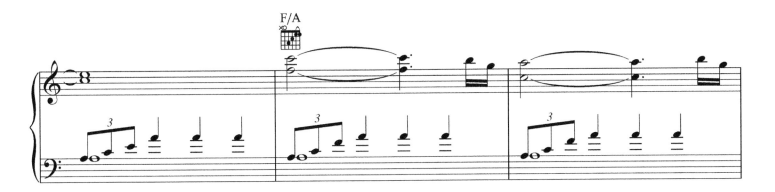

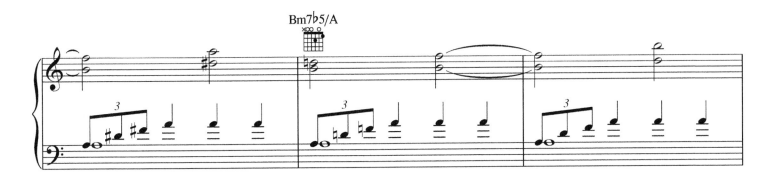

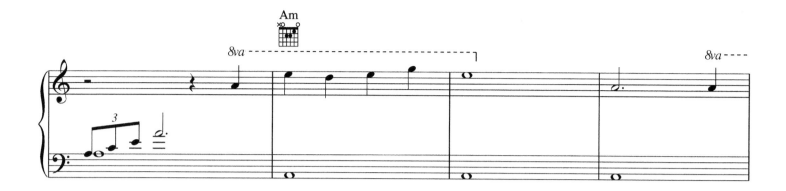

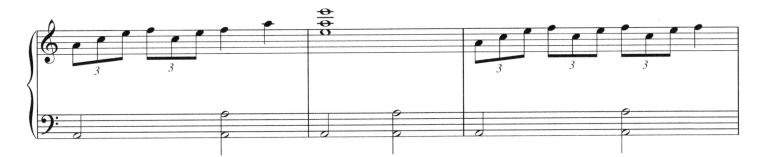

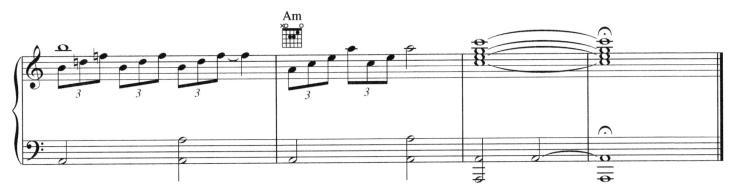

More Songbooks from Your Favorite Artists

ADELE – 30
12 songs: All Night Parking (Interlude) • Can I Get It • Can't Be Together • Cry Your Heart Out • Easy on Me • Hold On • I Drink Wine • Love Is a Game • My Little Love • Oh My God • Strangers by Nature • To Be Loved • Wild Wild West • Woman like Me.

00396758 Piano/Vocal/Guitar $19.99

JUSTIN BIEBER – JUSTICE
15 songs: Anyone • Die for You • Hold On • Holy • Lonely • Love You Different • Peaches • Somebody • Unstable • and more.

00368491 Piano/Vocal/Guitar $19.99

COLDPLAY – EVERYDAY LIFE
16 tracks featuring the title track plus: Arabesque • Broken • Champion of the World • Church • Cry Cry Cry • Daddy • Eko • Guns • Sunrise • When I Need a Friend • and more.

00327962 Piano/Vocal/Guitar $19.99

BILLIE EILISH – HAPPIER THAN EVER
15 songs: Billie Bossa Nova • Everybody Dies • Getting Older • Lost Cause • My Future • NDA • Therefore I Am • Your Power • and more.

00369297 Piano/Vocal/Guitar $19.99

FOO FIGHTERS – GREATEST HITS
15 songs: All My Life • Best of You • Big Me • Breakout • Everlong • Learn to Fly • Long Road to Ruin • Monkey Wrench • My Hero • The Pretender • Skin and Bones • This Is a Call • Times like These • Wheels • Word Forward • and more.

00142501 Piano/Vocal/Guitar..$22.99

ARIANA GRANDE – THANK U, NEXT
11 songs: Bad Idea • Bloodline • Break up with Your Girlfriend, I'm Bored • Fake Smile • Ghostin • Imagine • In My Head • Make Up • NASA • Needy • 7 Rings.

00292769 Piano/Vocal/Guitar $19.99

SHAWN MENDES – WONDER
14 songs: Always Been You • Call My Friends • Can't Imagine • Dream • Higher • Intro • Look up at the Stars • Monster • Piece of You • Song for No One • Teach Me How to Love • 305 • 24 Hours • Wonder.

00363568 Piano/Vocal/Guitar $19.99

MAREN MORRIS – SHEET MUSIC COLLECTION
15 songs: The Bones • Craving You • Dear Hate • 80s Mercedes • Girl • I Could Use a Love Song • The Middle • My Church • Rich • A Song for Everything • and more.

00319925 Piano/Vocal/Guitar $19.99

OLIVIA RODRIGO – SOUR
11 songs: Brutal • Deja Vu • Drivers License • Enough for You • Good 4 U • Happier • Hope Ur OK • Jealousy, Jealousy • Traitor • and more.

00369986 Piano/Vocal/Guitar $19.99

HARRY STYLES – HARRY'S HOUSE
13 songs: As It Was • Boyfriends • Cinema • Daydreaming • Daylight • Grapejuice • Keep Driving • Late Night Talking • Little Freak • Love of My Life • Matilda • Music for a Sushi Restaurant • Satellite.

01060060 Piano/Vocal/Guitar..$19.99

TAYLOR SWIFT – RED (TAYLOR'S VERSION)
29 songs: All Too Well (both versions!) • Better Man • Everything Has Changed • Holy Ground • I Knew You Were Trouble • Red • Sad Beautiful Tragic • State of Grace • 22 • We Are Never Ever Getting Back Together • and more.

00394706 Piano/Vocal/Guitar $27.99

HAL•LEONARD®

For a complete listing of the products available, visit us online at **www.halleonard.com**

Contents, prices, and availability subject to change without notice.

0822
015

Big Fun with Big-Note Piano Books!

These songbooks feature exciting easy arrangements for beginning piano students.

Beatles' Best
27 classics for beginners to enjoy, including: Can't Buy Me Love • Eleanor Rigby • Hey Jude • Michelle • Here, There and Everywhere • When I'm Sixty-Four • Yesterday • and more.
00222561..$14.99

The Best Songs Ever
70 favorites, featuring: Body and Soul • Crazy • Edelweiss • Fly Me to the Moon • Georgia on My Mind • Imagine • The Lady Is a Tramp • Memory • A String of Pearls • Tears in Heaven • Unforgettable • You Are So Beautiful • and more.
00310425..$19.95

Chart Hits of 2018-2019
15 of today's biggest hits. Songs include: Eastside (benny blanco with Halsey & Khalid) • High Hopes (Panic! At the Disco) • Sunflower (Post Malone & Swae Lee) • Without Me (Halsey) • and more.
00290100..$14.99

Children's Favorite Movie Songs
arranged by Phillip Keveren
16 favorites from films, including: The Bare Necessities • Beauty and the Beast • Can You Feel the Love Tonight • Do-Re-Mi • The Rainbow Connection • Tomorrow • Zip-A-Dee-Doo-Dah • and more.
00310838..$12.99

Disney Big-Note Collection
Over 40 Disney favorites, including: Circle of Life • Colors of the Wind • Hakuna Matata • It's a Small World • Under the Sea • A Whole New World • Winnie the Pooh • Zip-A-Dee-Doo-Dah • and more.
00316056..$19.99

Favorite Children's Songs
arranged by Bill Boyd
29 easy arrangements of songs to play and sing with children: Peter Cottontail • I Whistle a Happy Tune • It's a Small World • On the Good Ship Lollipop • The Rainbow Connection • and more!
00240251..$12.99

Favorite TV Themes
22 themes from the small screen, including: Addams Family Theme • Happy Days • Jeopardy Theme • Mission: Impossible Theme • Price Is Right (Opening Theme) • Sesame Street Theme • Won't You Be My Neighbor? • and more.
00294318..$10.99

Frozen
9 songs from this hit Disney film, plus full-color illustrations from the movie. Songs include the standout single "Let It Go", plus: Do You Want to Build a Snowman? • For the First Time in Forever • Reindeer(s) Are Better Than People • and more.
00126105..$12.99

The Great Big Book of Children's Songs – 2nd Edition
66 super tunes that kids adore, includes: Circle of Life • Edelweiss • If I Only Had a Brain • Over the Rainbow • Puff the Magic Dragon • Rubber Duckie • Sing • This Land Is Your Land • Under the Sea • and dozens more!
00119364..$17.99

Happy Birthday to You and Other Great Songs for Big-Note Piano
16 essential favorites, including: Chitty Chitty Bang Bang • Good Night • Happy Birthday to You • Heart and Soul • Over the Rainbow • Sing • This Land Is Your Land • and more.
00119636..$9.99

Modern Movie Favorites
Beginning pianists will love to play the 18 familiar movie hits in this collection, including: The Bare Necessities • Can't Stop the Feeling • City of Stars • How Far I'll Go • In Summer • Rey's Theme • Something Wild • and more.
00241880..$14.99

Pride & Prejudice
Music from the Motion Picture Soundtrack
12 piano pieces from the 2006 Oscar-nominated film: Another Dance • Darcy's Letter • Georgiana • Leaving Netherfield • Liz on Top of the World • Meryton Townhall • The Secret Life of Daydreams • Stars and Butterflies • and more.
00316125..$12.99

Songs of Peace, Hope and Love
30 inspirational and motivational songs, including: Bridge over Troubled Water • The Climb • Hallelujah • Over the Rainbow • Put a Little Love in Your Heart • What a Wonderful World • You Raise Me Up • and more.
00119634..$12.99

Star Wars
13 Selections from a Galaxy Far, Far Away
A baker's dozen of *Star Wars* selections by John Williams arranged by Phillip Keveren, include: Across the Stars (Love Theme from *Star Wars*) • The Imperial March (Darth Vader's Theme) • Luke and Leia • Rey's Theme • Star Wars (Main Theme) • and more.
00277371..$16.99

Today's Pop Hits – 3rd Edition
A great collection of current pop hits that even developing piano players will be able to enjoy. 15 songs with lyrics, including: All of Me • Happy • Hello • Pompeii • Radioactive • Roar • Shake It Off • Stay with Me • Story of My Life • and more.
00160577 ....$14.99

Top Hits of 2019
17 of the year's best are included in this collection for easy to read big note piano with lyrics: Gloria • I Don't Care • Lo/Hi • ME! • Old Town Road (Remix) • Senorita • Someone You Loved • Sucker • and more.
00302427..$14.99

The Big-Note Worship Book – 2nd Edition
20 selections for budding pianists looking to play their favorite worship songs: Everlasting God • Holy Is the Lord • In Christ Alone • Revelation Song • 10,000 Reasons (Bless the Lord) • Your Grace Is Enough • and more.
00267812..$12.99

HAL•LEONARD®

Complete song lists online at
www.halleonard.com

THE MOST REQUESTED SERIES

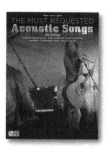

ACOUSTIC SONGS
48 songs: American Pie • Black Water • The Boxer • Cat's in the Cradle • Crazy Little Thing Called Love • Free Fallin' • Friend of the Devil • I Walk the Line • Landslide • More Than Words • Patience • Redemption Song • Summer Breeze • Toes • Wish You Were Here • and many more.

00001518 Piano/Vocal/Guitar $19.99

BOSSA NOVA & SAMBA SONGS
61 songs: Bonita • Don't Ever Go Away (Por Causa De Voce) • A Felicidade • The Girl from Ipanema (Garôta De Ipanema) • How Insensitive (Insensatez) • The Look of Love • Mas Que Nada • So Nice (Summer Samba) • Triste • and many more.

00154900 Piano/Vocal/Guitar $24.99

CHILDREN'S SONGS
73 songs: Addams Family Theme • Be Our Guest • Edelweiss • Ghostbusters • Happy Birthday to You • Linus and Lucy • Put on a Happy Face • Sing • So Long, Farewell • Take Me Out to the Ball Game • This Land Is Your Land • You Are My Sunshine • and many more.

00145525 Piano/Vocal/Guitar $19.99

CHRISTMAS SONGS
69 songs: Blue Christmas • Christmas Time Is Here • Deck the Hall • Feliz Navidad • Grandma Got Run over by a Reindeer • I'll Be Home for Christmas • Jingle Bells • Little Saint Nick • Nuttin' for Christmas • Rudolph the Red-Nosed Reindeer • Silent Night • and more.

00001563 Piano/Vocal/Guitar $24.99

CLASSIC ROCK SONGS
60 songs: Africa • Bang a Gong (Get It On) • Don't Stop Believin' • Feelin' Alright • Hello, It's Me • Layla • Life in the Fast Lane • Maybe I'm Amazed • Money • Only the Good Die Young • Small Town • Tiny Dancer • We Are the Champions • and more!

02501632 Piano/Vocal/Guitar $24.99

COUNTRY SONGS
47 songs: Cruise • Don't You Wanna Stay • Fly Over States • Gunpowder & Lead • How Do You Like Me Now?! • If I Die Young • Need You Now • Red Solo Cup • The Thunder Rolls • Wide Open Spaces • and more.

00127660 Piano/Vocal/Guitar $19.99

COUNTRY LOVE SONGS
59 songs: Always on My Mind • Amazed • Crazy • Forever and Ever, Amen • I Will Always Love You • Love Story • Stand by Your Man • Through the Years • When You Say Nothing at All • You're Still the One • and more.

00159649 Piano/Vocal/Guitar $29.99

FOLK/POP SONGS
62 songs: Blowin' in the Wind • Do You Believe in Magic • Fast Car • The House of the Rising Sun • If I Were a Carpenter • Leaving on a Jet Plane • Morning Has Broken • The Night They Drove Old Dixie Down • Puff the Magic Dragon • The Sound of Silence • Teach Your Children • and more.

00110225 Piano/Vocal/Guitar $22.99

ISLAND SONGS
60 songs: Beyond the Sea • Blue Hawaii • Coconut • Don't Worry, Be Happy • Electric Avenue • Escape (The Pina Colada Song) • I Can See Clearly Now • Island Girl • Kokomo • Redemption Song • Surfer Girl • Tiny Bubbles • and many more.

00197925 Piano/Vocal/Guitar $19.99

JAZZ STANDARDS
75 songs: All the Things You Are • Blue Skies • Embraceable You • Fascinating Rhythm • God Bless' the Child • I Got Rhythm • Mood Indigo • Pennies from Heaven • Satin Doll • Stella by Starlight • Summertime • The Very Thought of You • and more.

00102988 Piano/Vocal/Guitar $19.99

MOVIE SONGS
73 songs: Born Free • Chariots of Fire • Endless Love • I Will Always Love You • James Bond Theme • Mrs. Robinson • Moon River • Over the Rainbow • Stand by Me • Star Wars (Main Theme) • (I've Had) the Time of My Life • The Wind Beneath My Wings • and more!

00102882 Piano/Vocal/Guitar $19.99

POP/FOLK SONGS
60 songs: Alison • Annie's Song • Both Sides Now • The Boxer • California Girls • Fire and Rain • Joy to the World • Longer • Son-Of-A-Preacher Man • Summer in the City • Up on the Roof • and many more.

00145529 Piano/Vocal/Guitar $22.99

SONGS OF THE '60s
72 songs: Aquarius • The Beat Goes On • Beyond the Sea • Happy Together • Hey Jude • King of the Road • Like a Rolling Stone • Save the Last Dance for Me • Son-Of-A-Preacher Man • These Eyes • Under the Boardwalk • Up on the Roof • and more.

00110207 Piano/Vocal/Guitar $24.99

SONGS OF THE '70s
58 songs: Bohemian Rhapsody • Desperado • Hello, It's Me • I Will Survive • Just the Way You Are • Let It Be • Night Moves • Rocky Mountain High • Summer Breeze • Time in a Bottle • You're So Vain • Your Song • and many more.

00119714 Piano/Vocal/Guitar $24.99

SONGS OF THE '80s
59 songs: Africa • Billie Jean • Come on Eileen • Every Breath You Take • Faith • Footloose • Hello • Here I Go Again • Jessie's Girl • Like a Virgin • Livin' on a Prayer • Open Arms • Rosanna • Sweet Child O' Mine • Take on Me • Uptown Girl • and more.

00111668 Piano/Vocal/Guitar $27.99

SONGS OF THE '90s
51 songs: All I Wanna Do • ...Baby One More Time • Barely Breathing • Creep • Fields of Gold • From a Distance • Livin' La Vida Loca • Losing My Religion • Semi-Charmed Life • Smells like Teen Spirit • 3 AM • Under the Bridge • Who Will Save Your Soul • You Oughta Know • and more.

00111971 Piano/Vocal/Guitar $19.99

WEDDING RECEPTION SONGS
54 songs: Celebration • How Sweet It Is (To Be Loved by You) • Hungry Eyes • I Will Always Love You • In My Life • Isn't She Lovely • Last Dance • Let's Get It On • Love and Marriage • My Girl • Sunrise, Sunset • Unforgettable • The Way You Look Tonight • and more.

02501750 Piano/Vocal/Guitar $19.99

HAL•LEONARD®

www.halleonard.com
Prices, content, and availability subject to change without notice.

0422
080